Barnsley Libraries

CENTRAL

CW00268928

P.S.442

17/04/

Return Date

©Fitzwarren Publishing 2001

First published in 1995; Second edition 2001

British Library Cataloging in Publication Data
A CIP record for this book is available from the British Library.

ISBN 0-9524812 8 6

Published by: Fitzwarren Publishing,
2 Orchard Drive, Aston Clinton, Aylesbury, Bucks HP22 5HR

Printed in England by Halstan & Co. Ltd

CONTENTS

PREFACE

The landlord and tenant relationship is one which frequently draw parties into conflict. In any county court, at least one day a week will be devoted to possession actions. It is the most prolific area for contested litigation: more so than divorce, employment or consumer disputes.

Part of the reason for this is the fact that it involves two people owning what each would consider primarily theirs. The landlord, who has probably invested a lot of money and effort in a property, thinks of it as his subject to another person's temporary privilege of being able to live there. On the other hand, the tenant thinks of the same place as his home and the landlord's rights over it as very much secondary to his own.

Complicated legislation, which is often changed, attempts to regulate these respective claims. This combination of an inherently fraught situation and laws that many, including lawyers, do not entirely understand gives rise to so much litigation. Many subsequent problems can be avoided by following correct procedures at the stage of granting the tenancy. A fair proportion of landlord and tenant disputes are contested because someone has not followed the correct procedure.

Others arise because whilst there has been no "legal" error, the landlord has obviously not given any thought to the responsibility, let alone the risks, he has taken on by letting property. What this book tries to do is to guide both landlords and tenants through the problems and point out the responsibilities, legal and non-legal alike, of letting property.

There are several lawyers' practitioner texts, each one amounting to several volumes and thousands of pages. Whilst these are invaluable to some lawyers, for others - and in particular the general public - they are expensive, unwieldy, and difficult to navigate and understand.

This book was written to aid those who have an interest in residential tenancies - be they landlords, tenants, estate agents, managing agents or anyone else. It aims to fill the void that exists beneath the impenetrable legal tomes.

The first edition, published in 1995, was extremely successful, however since then a large number of changes have taken place in the area of residential tenancies and also to the general conduct of civil litigation.

This new edition takes into account these changes, both legal and practical. For example, the changes that affected the creation of assured shorthold tenancies after the implementation of the Housing Act, 1996, the gas and furniture regulations that all landlords, before letting their property must abide by, the Civil Procedure Rules that completely over-hauled the rules relating to civil procedure and practice and, not least, the impact of the Human Rights Act.

The simple format of the book remains, the text being divided into sections addressed to either side of the legal relationship - landlords and tenants. This edition does not stray from the roots of the last. However new legal and practical developments have occurred and the new edition ensures that those involved with residential tenancies remain up to date.

The main purpose of a preface is to acknowledge. I am extremely grateful to Alan Matthews (a pseudonym), the previous author of this book. The first edition was extremely successful and a large reason for its success was Alan's clear and lucid writing of the law that is, to many, confusing to say the least.

A large part of this book remains just as it was written in the first edition. I was (and remain) reluctant to discard text that remains coher-ent, articulate and unaffected by legal changes and have attempted to keep close to the origins of the first edition.

I also want to thank a number of people: to Alan Matthews, again, who provided me with the opportunity, advice and permission to use his text; to Mark Loveday, my first six pupil master who amongst many other things made this area of law interesting and navigable and who gave me the confidence, guidance and motivation to succeed at the Bar; to Julie Stretton, from the publishing side, who waited patiently for me to complete this work; and to Angie who allowed me the time to write this and encouraged me to do so when there seemed so many other more appealing options.

Finally, I remain forever indebted to my parents. Their encouragement and support throughout my study of the law will never be forgotten; without them, I know that I would never have attained even a fraction of what I have attained so far in my life.

1

INTRODUCTION

WHETHER TO RENT A PROPERTY

From the landlord's perspective

The number of private individuals letting property rose substantially in the 1990s. The main reason for this was the slump in house prices. Frequently people wishing to move realised that if they sold their home they would have to accept less than they had paid when they bought the property. Accordingly, many decided to buy new properties but rent their former homes while awaiting a turn around in the market.

This course had also been made more attractive by the provisions of the Housing Act 1988. The legislation in force before that Act meant that it was difficult for landlords to regain possession of their properties at the end of the terms for which they had been let. Further, the tenant was legally entitled to apply for a "fair rent" - usually be a fraction of the market rent. Horror stories abound of people who had let their homes supposedly for a few months at a substantial rent only to find that they had "sitting tenants" who could remain there for life paying a pittance.

Subsequent governments have sought to maintain the popularity of private lettings and they are now extremely common. For example, most students who study away from home rent privately whilst at university and many, as they move away from the family home, often rent as they do not have the funds to purchase a property of their own at the outset.

Before the changes made by the 1996 Housing Act there were stringent formalities that landlords had to comply with if they were not to run the risk of losing the right to recover their properties. Now, any tenancy granted after 28 February 1997 is, save certain exceptions, presumed to be an assured shorthold which provides the landlord with an easier method of recovery; although if a tenant refuses to leave at the end of the tenancy, the landlord will still need court proceedings.

This book looks at different types of tenancies. A protected tenancy or

Rent Act tenancy, i.e. a tenancy granted before 14 January 1989 (now becoming rarer and rarer); an assured tenancy or Housing Act tenancy, i.e. a tenancy granted after 14 January 1989.

Is the property suitable for letting?

Typically tenants will be young, single, not particularly well off and unlikely to see the property as being a permanent home. Often the same house will be shared by people who do not know each other very well. Such tenants may well spend less time at home than would a family. So, some factors which could substantially affect the value of a house when it is being sold may have less bearing on the rental value. These might include:

> *A quiet location*
> *Structural soundness*
> *Proximity of good schools*
> *Size of rooms*

However other factors might become more significant such as:

> *Proximity to local amenities such as shops and public transport (in London, being close to a tube station is particularly important)*
> *Number of rooms*
> *Having more than one bathroom/shower room and a separate toilet*

Annual rents very roughly average around 10% of properties freehold (or in the case of flats, long leasehold) value. Two hypothetical examples may illustrate these principles:

1. 41a Wilson Road, Stratford, London E15

This is a four bedroom flat with a lounge, bathroom, kitchen and separate toilet, above shops on a major road, five minutes walk from Stratford British Rail and tube station. Such a flat might sell for about £150,000. Applying the 10% principle, the starting point for the rent would be around £15,000 per year. However because of the number of rooms it is likely that at least four tenants would live there. The separate toilet would make communal living a little easier than if they all had to share. They would be attracted all the more because of the flat being near the shops and particularly the tube.

It would not be difficult to find people willing to pay at least £80 per week each to live in such a flat. That translates into a rent of £320 per week or around £16,600 per year.

2. Heath Cottage, Aldenham, Herts

This is a two bedroom cottage with a through lounge in a south Hertfordshire village to which there is little public transport. If it were sold it would probably be worth around £125,000. However finding tenants willing to pay £12,500 per year for it could prove very difficult. It would be ideal for a couple with a young child.

However if such people are able to afford a rent of about £240 per week, they would probably prefer to buy a place of their own. In this situation the landlord may well have to settle for a rent less than 10%, say around £8,000 per year, or around £154 per week.

Another factor which affects whether or not renting is likely to be profitable is the level of mortgage interest rates. At the time of writing these are around 6%. Most privately-owned properties will be mortgaged to banks or building societies. The amount of interest payable on that mortgage will have to be balanced against the rent received. If the mortgage is less than 100% of the value of the home the landlord will have to take into account the notional amount of income he would be receiving were he to invest the surplus after repaying the mortgage he would get on sale.

On the other hand, some mortgages amount to more than 100% of the value of the property. This syndrome, often known as "negative equity", arises where the value of a property falls after it has been mortgaged, making the amount of money secured on it more than the property is worth. In this situation the prospective landlord also has to consider the amount of interest he would have to pay on money he borrowed to enable him to repay the mortgage.

As he would no longer have the property on which to secure that loan, he would almost certainly pay a rate higher than was charged under the mortgage. This can be illustrated by looking at the positions of the owners of the above examples.

1. Mrs Healey

Mrs Healey owns 41a Wilson Road. She bought the flat at the height of the "boom" for £163,000 with 100% mortgage. Interest on her mortgage is around £10,000: much less than the rent she would receive. If she sold the flat for £150,000 she would still have to pay interest on the £13,000 shortfall. On an unsecured loan of that amount she might have to pay 15%, an annual sum of around £2,000. Thus she would only be reducing her payments by £8,000 (£10,000 less £2,000) if she sold the flat, which is substantially less than she would receive per year by way of rent.

2. Mr Barber

Mr Barber owns Heath Cottage, worth around £125,000. He only has a £100,000 mortgage on it, on which he pays £6,000 per year. Mr Barber calculates that if sold the property and put the equity in a building society he would receive £1,250 a year in interest, and would save himself £6,000 a year in mortgage payments. He would therefore be saving £7,250, only £750 less than he might be receiving per year in rent. In the event he decides to sell.

Mrs Healey, therefore, would be well advised to let her property and decides she will do so. Her property will form the basis of a number of examples throughout this book. For the sake of keeping a small cast, this book will haveMr Barber sell to Mrs Healey. She will go and live there and in due course decide to let the spare bedroom.

Landlords inevitably have to pay other expenses. Insurance of the property (though not the contents), water rates and most repairs are the landlord's responsibility in a normal residential tenancy. Depending on the area and the condition of the premises these might take up 15% of the rent. Some landlords may elect to use agents to find tenants in the first place and to subsequently manage the property. Fees, particularly for managing the property, can be substantial. The advantages and disadvantages of using agents are discussed elsewhere in this book.

To keep the examples given above as simple as possible no account has been taken of the cost of furnishing the properties. This aspect is discussed in later pages. The provision of furniture is rarely more than a marginal cost to the landlord compared with those connected with the property itself.

When considering mortgage repayments, the above examples were also restricted to interest. There will in practice either be a capital repayment to be made along with the interest or a premium on the endowment policy. In the long term these payments can be disregarded as the landlord is "buying" something with them, either a capital interest in the property itself or the benefit of the endowment (although, following the recent endowment fiasco, "benefit" may be too generous a word to use). However, for a person with cash flow difficulties, being released from the need to make those payments may be a welcome relief.

It should also be borne in mind that a rental income can never be completely secure. There is always the possibility that the tenants will fail to pay the rent, damage the property or cause the landlord to run up substantial legal fees to get them out. If these things happen, the bank lending money on the property will show scant sympathy to a landlord who as a result defaults on his mortgage repayments.

If despite all this the landlord does make a profit on renting the property, he will have to pay tax on it.

With all these factors in mind Mr Barber would seem to have very little to gain by renting out Heath Cottage. Inevitably, his expenses would be greater than the rental income. Probably the capital value of the property will increase over the next few years, though the chances are it will not do so to such an extent as to cancel out his losses.

On the other hand Mrs Healey will almost certainly be better off renting rather than selling 41a Wilson Road: even after paying all possible expenses including agents if she chooses to use them, she will make a few thousand pounds profit per year.

From the tenant's perspective

For many tenants the decision whether to rent or buy is made for them by the banks and building societies who will not advance them enough money to buy. As we noted earlier, the typical tenant is likely to be young and single and does not see property as a long term home. It should at this point be pointed out that this book is concerned only with privately let homes. Council housing of course provides secure homes for many millions of families.

Whilst the factors that might affect whether someone sells or lets property are primarily financial, the decision from the point of the view of the prospective tenant will be far more influenced by personal matters.

As a result of the massive rise in housing prices over recent years home ownership is for many, once again, inaccessible. Since the first edition of this book in 1995 housing prices have dramatically increased, and whereas five years ago home-ownership was more accessible because of the fall in housing prices, this is far from the present case.

It appears that housing prices have now to some extent stabilised and in some areas are even falling. In spite of the fact that (in London at the very least) there are housing and flat developments seemingly on every other street, there is nevertheless now becoming less and less reasonably priced accommodation available. It is now common for a two bed-roomed flat in London to cost over £100,000. Unfortunately, wages have not grown at a similar rate to housing prices and so with mortgages of three times an individual's or two and a half times a couple's joint salary, buying a home is becoming less of a viable option.

Applying the principles discussed in relation to landlords with mortgage interest rates around 6% and a typical rent 10% of a property's value, buying is likely to be more attractive if it is possible to get a mortgage and financial factors alone are taken into account. Even bearing in mind the other costs, such as insurance, repairs, water rates and capital repayments, owning a home will generally cost no more than renting the same home over an extended period.

However, it should be borne in mind that mortgage rates fluctuate. It was not too long ago that mortgage rates were virtually double what they are at the time of writing. There is little agreement amongst economists as to whether they are more likely to go up or down in the next few years but there is certainly more scope for them to go substantially up rather than substantially down. Although rents to some extent follow mortgage interest rates the degree of fluctuation is much less.

It may also be possible for someone who has bought a property to offset some of the cost by letting a room in it to a lodger, a course which is discussed elsewhere in this book.

Whatever the financial issues, it has to be remembered that home-ownership involves a tremendous commitment. Many young people enjoy the freedom of being able to move around with relatively few constraints. They may find a job in a different part of the country, move in with a partner or simply become tired of their present environment and want to live in a different area. With rented property there is unlikely to be a tie preventing them from moving after more than a few months. Selling a property often takes far longer.

Stories abound of the misery of separated couples who cannot sell their property and are forced to continue living together, sometimes sharing the only bedroom and even platonic friends can fall out. Only if you are very sure of your relationship should you consider buying a property with someone to whom you are not married or, at least, in a serious relationship.

Arrangements between brothers and sisters who purchase properties together often work reasonably well. Whilst they will have as many rows as any other sharers, the underlying relationship is likely to be strong enough to prevent them seriously falling out. And the prospects of parental help is substantially enhanced when a property is going to remain entirely within the family.

Many people do not like the idea of living alone. Having flatmates should on the whole be pleasant, providing someone with whom to share the chores as well as someone to talk to in the evenings. Many shared households become almost surrogate families.

Buying and selling can also be an expensive business. Solicitors' fees are likely to be at least £350 for both the buyer and seller. A survey might also cost the buyer that much. When a property is sold estate agents tend to charge around 1.5%.

If the price is over £60,000, 1% stamp duty has to be paid by the buyer. If a person has owned a property for less than two or so years before selling it these costs are likely to amount to more than the saving made had the person rented a similar property over the same period.

2

GRANTING THE TENANCY

PRELIMINARY CONSIDERATIONS

From the landlord's perspective

Before granting the tenancy the landlord should consider the legal implications what he is doing. This is when he should take professional advice or at very least triple check that he has done everything correctly. It is easier and cheaper to avoid mistakes now than to put them right later. From some points of view granting a tenancy is just as big a step as selling a house. Almost everybody selling a house appreciates the significance of the transaction and has at least a vague idea of the dangers involved. In many ways renting is an even riskier business. More landlords suffer because of badly prepared tenancy agreements than do sellers (or purchasers) because of conveyancing problems.

Most landlords will want to ensure that they can regain possession of the property at the end of the agreed term of the tenancy. Before the 28 February 1997 this was relatively straightforward providing that the landlord could get the paperwork right before granting the tenancy. Matters of detail were absolutely essential. It was possible for a landlord to find that he had given a tenant the right to remain in the property for the rest of his life simply because a prescribed notice was in the wrong form or because it was handed over too late.

Now, it is has become easier for landlords to regain possession. From 28 February 1997 all new tenancies are assured shorthold tenancies without the need for any further formality. The exacting need for precision in a notice has disappeared and it is not now necessary to serve any notice before the tenancy begins.

Although any tenant has the entitlement to a written statement of the terms of the tenancy, there is no legal requirement for a tenancy to be granted by a written document (unless the tenancy is for more than three years where it is essential). It can be done orally. That, however, is a course which from the landlord's point of view has little to recommend it. Written agreements and notices are generally prepared by landlords with a view to protecting their interests. If these are dispensed with, the landlord will have lost his opportunity to protect himself, as well as failed to ensure there is an easily provable record of precisely what was agreed between him and the tenant.

A landlord will only have a duty to provide his tenant with a statement of the terms of the tenancy if the tenancy is an assured shorthold and he is asked, in writing, to do so.

The duty of the landlord, in this scenario, is to provide information on:

a) the date upon which the tenancy began

b) the amount of the rent

c) when the rent is payable

d) details of any rent review

e) the length of the term, if the tenancy is for a fixed term,

Somewhat strangely, however, this statement is not to be regarded as conclusive evidence as to the original agreement between the parties. Thus, for example, simply because the landlord makes a mistake over the amount of rent, he is not necessarily prevented from asking for the amount originally agreed. A landlord who, without reasonable excuse, fails to comply within 28 days to a tenant's request for the terms of the tenancy is liable to be fined up to £2,500 in the magistrates' court.

Assured shorthold tenancies

The granting of assured shorthold tenancies is the most widely used way by which landlords ensure that they can get the property back. As we have noted, virtually all tenancies granted after 28 February 1997 are assured shorthold tenancies. One of the fundamental differences between an assured shorthold tenancy granted now and one arranged before 1997 is that there is no longer any necessity to give a notice in a prescribed form. Neither is there is a limitation on the type or length of the term (although a landlord cannot seek possession until at least 6 months have expired from the date the tenancy began)

An assured tenancy that was granted before 28 February 1997 can only be an assured shorthold if it was a residential tenancy for six months or longer and the landlord served the correct notice. The landlord must have served a notice on the tenant that the tenancy was to be an assured shorthold before the tenancy was entered into, i.e. before a binding tenancy agreement was made. He could not wait until the tenant started living in the property.

On the notice, the landlord must have inserted the address of the property, the starting date and length of the tenancy, the date the notice was served, the parties' names and the landlord's address - any inaccuracy in the notice would be likely to render it invalid (even a misspelling of the landlord's name has made a notice invalid!).

If there was more than one tenant, the notice must have been addressed to both or all of them. A copy of the notice should have been kept and, ideally, the tenant would write on the copy a statement that he had received the original. Only once that had been done could the landlord and tenant/tenants sign the main tenancy agreement so that an assured shorthold tenancy (under the old regime) could be created. There is, now - certainly on the part of landlords and managing agents - a sense of relief that these essential details are no longer necessary.

Exceptions

There are some categories which exclude the creation of an assured tenancy (although other statutory protection is likely to apply). The most important exclusions are:-

> *Tenancies entered into before 15 January 1989*
> *A resident landlord*
> *If the rent is very high - over £25,000 per year*
> *If the rent is very low - less than £1,000 if the dwelling is located in Greater London, and £250 anywhere else*
> *If the landlord is the Crown, a government department, a local authority, a housing association*
> *If there is a business tenancy to which the Landlord and Tenant Act 1954 applies (If there is mixed residential and business premises it is likely that the tenant will not have an assured tenancy, but it is a matter where expert advice should be sought)*
> *If the purpose of the tenancy is to give the tenant a right to occupy the dwelling-house for a holiday*
> *Tenancies of agricultural land (where the land exceeds two acres)*

Tenancies of licensed premises (ie: a pub)

The landlord's home

Where the landlord has previously lived in the property as his only or principal home or he intends to do so in the future, he can grant a Ground 1 tenancy (after Ground 1 of Schedule 2 to the Housing Act 1988). This form of tenancy is not used by landlords, even landlords entitled to grant them, with anything like so much frequency as are assured shorthold tenancies.

The main advantage to a Ground 1 tenancy is that the landlord has more flexibility in subsequently increasing the rent. Where the landlord has not previously lived in the property, granting the tenancy on the basis that the landlord intends to live there in future is obviously a potentially dangerous course. If he changes his mind and decides not to live in the property after all, he will have no way of forcing the tenant out.

A landlord granting a Ground 1 tenancy must serve a notice on the tenant before the beginning of the tenancy that possession may be recovered pursuant to that Ground. Again if there is more than one tenant, it must be served on all of them. This notice does not have to follow any particular wording.

Returning to the example of Mrs Healey and 41a Wilson Road, she has lived in the property and might well decide to grant a tenancy of this sort rather than an assured shorthold tenancy. She must first prepare the following notice, leaving spaces for the insertion of relevant details including the tenant's acknowledgement of receipt.

To ....

This is to give you notice that I have previously occupied 41a Wilson Road, Stratford, London E15 as my only or principal home. Therefore the tenancy you intend taking of this property will be subject to Ground 1 of Schedule 2 to the Housing Act 1988 and I will be able to recover possession pursuant to that notice.

Signed: A H Healey (Mrs) landlord
Date: .. / .. / 20..

I have received a copy of this notice on [insert date .. /.. / 20..]before being granted any tenancy of 41a Wilson Road

Signed: .... **tenant**

Mrs Healey would then prepare the tenancy agreement.

Other ways of avoiding giving security of tenure

There are several other methods prescribed in Schedule 2 to the Housing Act 1988 that a landlord may use to avoid granting a tenancy giving security of tenure. The one that is likely to affect private landlords is Ground 3.This applies if the tenancy is for a specified period of up to eight months and in the previous twelve months the property had been occupied under a right to occupy it for a holiday.

Under this Ground 3 notification similar to a Ground 1 notice has to be served. It should be noted that if the letting is granted for the purpose of enabling the tenant to occupy the property for a holiday no security of tenure will be given. Educational establishments and religious bodies and ministers are also able in some circumstances to grant tenancies which will not attract security.

Licences

People are sometimes granted a licence to live in a property rather than a tenancy of the property. Where that happens a completely different nomenclature is used. Landlord becomes "licensor"; tenant "licensee"; rent, "licence fee". Someone living in another person's home as a lodger is clearly a licensee rather than a tenant. However, where the right to live in an entire property is granted to a person or a group of people such a right is generally regarded as a tenancy rather than a licence, even if the landlord made the tenant sign an agreement saying it was a licence.

Before the passing of the Housing Act 1988 landlords had fewer means of avoiding the legislation (the Rent Act 1977) giving tenants considerable rights. Accordingly, the use of licence agreements was common. Until 1985 the courts were surprisingly willing to uphold such agreements even in cases where objectively there would have appeared to be a tenancy.

However, in 1985 the judicial House of Lords set a precedent in considering an agreement entered into between a 'Mr Street' and a 'Mrs Mountford'. Under this agreement Mrs Mountford was granted a "licence" to live in a furnished room in Bournemouth. However, the Lords notwithstanding that description decided it was in fact a tenancy. Mrs Mountford had been granted exclusive possession of that room: the landlord could not require her to share it with anybody else. That factor (exclusive possession) was all important and prevented the landlord from being able to avoid the Rent Act.

There are still a few situations where a licence will have been granted. The most obvious and important example is that of a lodger. Where one person lets another live in property for the purpose of him being able to do his job that too will be a licence, known as a service licence or service occupancy, not a tenancy. An example of this would be a caretaker living in the block of flats he looks after.

The grey area is where a landlord lets a house to a number of different people at different times for different periods. If the people living there are left to decide amongst themselves who is to sleep in which room, there is arguably no identifiable piece of property that each could be said to have been granted a tenancy of.

Since the Housing Act 1988 was passed there has been little point in landlords claiming that what they have granted is not a tenancy. Any attempt to do so will be fraught with danger. If a dispute arises and the landlord fails to persuade the court that the agreement actually is a licence, he will have lost his opportunity to grant an assured shorthold tenancy rather than one which permits the tenants to stay indefinitely.

Company lets

Where a property is let to a limited company rather than an individual the rights given to tenants under the Housing Act 1988 will not apply. Before the Housing Act 1988 such lets were often used as a means to avoid the Rent Act. The would-be tenant would be required to form or purchase a company and the landlord would grant the tenancy to that company, which as tenant would allow its owner to live in the property. This, like the licence, is a device fraught with difficulties that landlords would now be well advised to avoid. If it subsequently appeared that the real intention was to grant a tenancy to the individual, a court might consider that there actually was a tenancy in favour of that individual.

There are however also genuine company lets under which an established company takes a tenancy of a property which it in turn lets to an employee or director. Such a letting will be outside the Housing Act 1988. The only disadvantage to the landlord in such a letting is that if the company goes into liquidation it will not be possible to recover any arrears of rent.

The length of the tenancy

After deciding on the type of tenancy, the landlord will have to decide on its length. He may not find tenants willing to accept a tenancy for the term he has in mind and may have to accept something less than ideal. Generally speaking it is unwise to put pressure on tenants to enter into agreements for longer than they want. However reprehensible it may be, tenants will often simply leave with no forwarding address and owing rent if they are under an obligation to stay once they want to go.

The landlord should ensure that he does not grant such a long tenancy that he cannot sell or live in the property when he wishes to do so. On the other hand he will not want to grant such a short tenancy that the tenants may be gone in a few weeks and he has to find replacements.

A tenancy can be for as short a term as the landlord wants. Many tenancies are in fact not for a set term at all. Instead they are granted from week to week or month to month - occasionally from quarter to quarter or year to year and can be ended by the giving of notice on either side. (It should, though, be remembered that giving notice will not entitle the landlord to possession unless he can show that there is a statutory Ground for possession as well)

The 1996 Housing Act which amended the 1988 Act now means that there is no minimum term which needs to be granted for there to be an assured shorthold; however, a landlord will not be able to seek possession until at least six months have expired since the tenancy started.

A landlord who is unsure of the length of time for which he wants to let a property can try to persuade the tenant to accept an agreement for a specific length of time which contains a break clause. This clause means the landlord can, on serving the appropriate notice to quit, bring the tenancy to an end within the term. It is also possible for a tenant to be

14

able to take advantage of a break clause. However a break clause is rarely worded to provide this benefit.

The rent

Factors that are likely to affect the rent are discussed elsewhere but a starting point for calculating rent might be 10% of the freehold value of the property. If this approach is to be used, it is first necessary to find out roughly what the freehold value is. Most estate agents will provide a free oral valuation. In quiet times some will not even be put off doing so if told the truth: that the owner is not at the moment considering selling.

They will provide information in the hope that when the property is eventually sold the help they have previously provided is remembered. Indeed some will even be prepared to give an informed view of the likely market rent. Of course, a landlord using an agency to let the property will have the benefit of that agency's experience of local conditions in assessing the rent.

The 10% figure even in conjunction with the other factors discussed later provides only a very rough indication. A look in local newspapers at the rents being sought for comparable properties will provide a more reliable guide. A prospective   landlord   who   knows   others   renting property in the area will be able get information from them about rent levels.

Joint landlords

If a property is jointly owned by more than one person, the principles relating to letting are much as the same as a property in single ownership. Ideally all documents should be signed by both owners. However if that causes difficulties one landlord can sign on behalf of both. This applies to initial notices, the tenancy agreement and any notices that may have to be served later under the tenancy itself.

Joint tenants

Most properties are let to more than one tenant. Tenancy agreements normally have the effect of making joint tenants jointly and severally liable to observe the obligations of the lease and pay the rent. The most important implication of this is that if one moves out, the other(s) must continue to pay the entire rent. If the landlord enters into separate agreements with each tenant, then each can only be liable in respect of his share of the obligations. Whilst doing this may prevent there being an assured tenancy altogether, it can cause confusion and uncertainty.

Once tenants have become established in a property it is not a good idea for the landlord to decide who moves in with them if one of their number leaves. Granting the lease to all the tenants jointly protects the landlord's position as far as payment of rent is concerned and gives the tenants more autonomy in deciding matters such as who should live in the property. Where there is more than one tenant, all notices must be addressed to, and where appropriate acknowledged by, all of the tenants.

Was the tenancy granted after 14 January 1989?
In most cases it will be obvious when the tenancy was granted. However there are a few situations in which the law may deem the tenancy to have been granted before 14 January 1989 and hence subject to the rules of the Rent Act 1977 which are generally less favourable to landlords than the Housing Act 1988. If the tenancy agreement was made before that date, then the tenancy will be subject to the Rent Act regardless of when it actually started.

A landlord who lets property to a person previously his tenant under a Rent Act tenancy will create another tenancy that is still subject to the Rent Act 1977 even if it were granted after 14 January 1989. This applies regardless of whether the tenancy is in respect of a different property, whether the landlord grants the tenancy jointly with another landlord or jointly to another tenant. The only exception to this provision is if the earlier tenancy was or had been a protected shorthold tenancy.

Was the tenancy granted after 28 February 1997?
As in the scenario above, if the tenancy agreement was made before 28 February 1997 and the landlord failed to inform the tenant before the tenancy began that the tenancy was to be a shorthold tenancy (a Section 20 notice), then the tenancy is likely to be an assured tenancy. In most other cases, whether there is a formal notice or not, the tenancy will be a shorthold tenancy.

Deposits
It is the normal practice for a landlord to seek a deposit of between a fortnight's and two months' rent from his tenants. This gives the landlord

a simple means of compensating himself if the tenants leave without paying their rent or if they cause damage at the property. It is a good idea to incorporate into the tenancy agreement a statement of what the deposit is designed to secure against, and also for it to state that the tenants may not recover the deposit by simply failing to pay their final instalments of rent.

An inventory of the landlord's property including fixtures and fittings, and furniture if appropriate, is usually drawn up. This can be done by the landlord himself. If anything is already broken or worn at the time the tenancy is granted, this should be noted on the inventory. The tenants should be given an opportunity to make a thorough inspection of the premises before signing the inventory. When agents deal with letting they generally use a specialist inventory clerk. A landlord may find it worthwhile to employ such a person: the resulting inventory is likely to be much more authoritative in the event of a subsequent dispute than one drawn up by the landlord himself.

It is advisable to insist on the deposit being paid and, if the payment is by cheque, that it is cleared before the tenants move in. However, the landlord should remember that the deposit is intended as a security and not as an interest free loan by the tenant to him. The landlord is under a moral and legal duty to pay any interest the deposit has earned to the tenant. This will usually not be a very large sum. Over the course of a year a deposit of £500 will probably only attract about £30 interest. Agreeing to pay this over will however show the tenants that the landlord intends to play fair: something that will often generate goodwill worth a lot more than £30.

References

Making some checks on a tenant's reliability is advisable. The most frequent sources of such information are employers or colleges, banks and previous landlords but obtaining references from any of these sources can be difficult. Previous landlords will more often than not fail to reply. Banks' replies have to be expressed in very non-committal terms to avoid the possibility of breaching confidence or of saying something about which either the landlord or tenant might have a sustainable complaint. An employer's reference is likely to do no more than establish that the tenant works for whom he claims.

A stamped addressed envelope is a courtesy that will increase the chances of obtaining a reply from a previous landlord or an employer. If the landlord approaches a bank, they will not disclose any information without their customer's permission. A prospective tenant will have to sign his consent which should be sent with the reference request. There is no harm in a copy of this being sent to the previous landlord and employer.

A previous landlord's reference referring to late payment of rent and raising other complaints about the tenant may well put most landlords off but it could be unfair to deprive a person of the opportunity of home because he is overdrawn or has only recently taken on a new job.

It may sometimes be possible to obtain references over the telephone, although banks will require an approach in writing. (Many will refuse to accept even a fax for this purpose, insisting on an "original" signature)

Just as effective as references in many cases is the production of documents by the tenant. If he can produce pay slips, bank statements and a rent book showing satisfactory finances over the last few months that is at least as effective as seeking that information from the people he has been dealing with. It will certainly be a lot quicker.

Replies to requests for references inevitably take a while. If the landlord is not prepared to commit himself to granting a tenancy during that period, the tenant can hardly be blamed for looking elsewhere. There is little point in granting a tenancy, before checking references since the granting of the tenancy is irrevocable, unsatisfactory references being no basis upon which to obtain possession.

At 41a Wilson Road Mrs Healey has decided that she will insist on written references. To save time once she starts meeting prospective tenants she has prepared letters in advance, leaving details particular to the tenant and the date yet to be filled in before sending them.

> *To the bank*
> Dear Sir,
> Re: [Name of tenant] and a/c no
> I understand [name of tenant] keeps the above account at your branch. He/she wishes to rent a flat from me at a rent of £320 per week, which he/she will share with three other tenants. I wonder if you could tell me whether he/she is

good for such an amount? A prompt reply would be appreciated.
Yours faithfully,

To the previous landlord
Dear Sir,
Re: [Name of tenant] and the tenancy of [tenant's present address]
I understand [name of tenant] has been a tenant of the above property of which you are landlord since [date]. I wonder if you could confirm that that is the case and that he/she has been a satisfactory tenant? I enclose a stamped addressed envelope. A prompt reply would be appreciated.
Yours faithfully,

To the employer
Dear Sir,
Re: [name of tenant]
I understand that [name of tenant] has worked for you as a [tenant's job] for you since [date]April 2000 and that he/she is paid a gross sum of [tenant's wages or salary]. He/she wishes to rent a flat from me and I would be grateful if you would confirm this information is correct. I enclose a stamped addressed envelope. A prompt reply would be appreciated.
Yours faithfully,

Consent form
To whom it may concern:
I hereby give consent to the disclosure to Mrs A H Healey of any financial or other information requested by way of reference as to whether or not she would be advised to grant me a tenancy of a residential property.

Sureties
Once a tenant has left a property, it is all but impossible to recoup rent

from him. If he leaves the property substantially in arrears, he probably will not tell the landlord of his new address. Where the landlord has taken a deposit there will be something to offset against the arrears, but it often will not be sufficient, especially if damage has also been caused. Even if a recalcitrant former tenant can be traced, he may not be in a position to repay outstanding sums. Suing him is likely to result in "good money" being thrown after "bad".

A landlord can greatly reduce the risk of this happening by insisting that the tenant provide a surety for the rent. This means that someone else promises the landlord that the tenant will pay the rent and any other sums owing as a result of the tenancy agreement and agrees to pay those sums if the tenant defaults on them. Typically, the surety will be the tenant's parents, though sometimes employers and friends are willing to take on the job. As well as providing the landlord with a remedy if anything goes wrong, the knowledge that their parents will become involved if they misbehave is enough to make many tenants act responsibly.

For a surety agreement to be valid, it has to be in writing and signed by the surety. It is also essential that the agreement is made before there is a binding tenancy. If it is not, the surety has not received any benefit and will not be bound by his promise to pay if the tenant defaults. It is a good idea to suggest the surety seek legal advice as there is a possibility if the surety signed the agreement without being given an opportunity to understand it, then the agreement would not be enforceable.

> *The surety agreement Mrs Healey prepared for her tenant's sureties, whom she imagined would be his parents ran:*
>
> In consideration for the grant of a tenancy of 41a Wilson Road, Stratford, London E15 by Mrs A H Healey to [tenant's name]. I hereby agree to indemnify Mrs A H Healey against any default in payment of rent, mesne profits, damages for use and occupation, damages for disrepair, other damages or costs she may incur as a result of the said tenancy or any further occupation of the property after the expiry of the tenancy whether under a statutory continuation thereof or not.
> Signed ....
> Witnessed ....

Mrs Healey prepared a covering letter for sending to the sureties:

Dear Mr/Mrs [name],
I understand from your son/daughter [tenant's name] that you are willing to stand surety if I grant him/her a tenancy of 41a Wilson Road, Stratford, London E15. I enclose a blank surety form for your and a witness' signature. Could I point out that this does potentially entail a substantial liability if [tenant's name] should default and you might think it appropriate to seek the advice of a solicitor before signing it.
Yours sincerely,

Even the existence of a surety cannot provide an absolute guarantee against the tenant's default. It may turn out that his parents, despite their 'posh' sounding address, are no better off than their son/daughter. It would be possible to ask the sureties to provide references as in the case of tenants but many would refuse to do this, feeling they have done their bit by agreeing to be sureties at all.

An important notice

A landlord has to serve a notice on the tenant giving the tenant an address at which notices relating to the tenancy can be served on him. This address must be in England or Wales. Landlords living abroad will have to provide the address of an agent, who can be a friend or professional adviser, for this purpose. If this notice is not served, the landlord is not entitled to any rent until he does serve it.

It has been held by the Court of Appeal that stating the address in the lease is sufficient to comply with this obligation. However the position is still far from clear, and landlords would be well advised to serve a notice separately when granting a new tenancy.

Similarly, if a notice has not already been served during the currency of an existing tenancy, sending one to a tenant could protect the landlord's position if he has the slightest reason to think the tenant may ever default. A person who demands or receives rent and, without reasonable cause, fails to supply the landlord's name and address within 21 days of any written request is committing an offence and is liable to be fined up to £2,500.

> *The notice Mrs Healey prepared to give her tenants read as follows:*
> To:
> The tenant [or tenants], [tenant's name or names]:
> This notice is to inform you that all notices (including notices in proceedings) may be served on me at the following address:
> Heath Cottage,
> Aldenham,
> Hertfordshire
>
> This notice is intended to and does comply with the requirements of s48 of the Landlord and Tenant Act 1987.
> Signed A H Healey (Mrs) The landlord

Other charges

A landlord inevitably incurs other costs in granting a tenancy. He may have had to advertise for tenants; he may have paid a solicitor to check the tenancy agreement for him; he may have employed an inventory clerk. Landlords do sometimes try to pass on some or all of these costs to the tenants at the start of the lease. Doing this was a criminal offence under the Rent Act 1977. Since the Housing Act 1988 came into force the landlord is entitled to charge the tenants a premium, which is what reimbursement for expenses amounts to. However, it remains a some-what unsavoury practice. Tenants resent it and understandably so.

In some circumstances, payment of a premium may entitle the tenant to transfer the tenancy to another without the landlord's permission. If the landlord is determined to recover his expenses, he should adjust the rent appropriately. If he cannot find anyone willing to pay the enhanced rent he may not have found anyone willing to pay the premium.

Repairs

To a large extent the rules on repairing obligations are ordained by statute (section 11 of the Landlord and Tenant Act 1985). Only leases of seven years or longer are excluded from these provisions. In essence, the landlord is responsible for:

· the exterior of the property
· all structural repairs
· maintaining the plumbing
· repairs to baths, sinks, basins and other sanitary installations
· space and water heating
· electricity, sanitation, gas and water supplies

These are the landlords responsibilities and they cannot be excluded in an agreement between landlord and tenant. However, there is a power for the parties to make a joint application to the court for an order that excludes or varies them (though it is difficult to envisage any good reason for a tenant to want to exclude or vary the landlords responsibilities for repairing the property in which the tenant will live).

Any attempt by the landlord to place these repairing obligations onto the tenant will be void. However, the responsibility for repairs other than those mentioned above depend on what agreements are made with the tenant. Thus, there is no reason why the landlord cannot require the tenants to be responsible for maintaining the decoration at the premises, although this may be hard to enforce. In a lease for more than around three years it would be reasonable to require the tenants to decorate the property in the last three months of the term.

In theory if the lease is silent on the point, tenants are under a duty to carry out repairs which are not specified by the Landlord and Tenant Act to be the landlord's responsibility (i.e. those listed above).

Other terms of the lease

A number of provisions that protect a landlord's interests are virtually standard in leases. Few are likely to be objected to by tenants. However there are a few further matters the landlord should consider before the tenancy agreement is completed. He must remember that once tenants have moved in it is their home and he can no longer make up rules. It is therefore vital that he imposes them at this stage and incorporates them into the agreement.

Does he wish to restrict the number of people who can live or sleep in the property? Once the lease is granted there is nothing to stop the original tenant having other people move in with him. A landlord may have let a property to an individual or a couple only to find there are four or five people living there. This may well result in a great deal more wear and tear on the property than would have been caused by a single tenant. A large and fluctuating body of overnight guests is likely to have a similarly undesirable effect. A clause in the lease imposing some sort of restriction might be advisable.

Does the landlord object to pets? It would usually be wise to include a prohibition on the keeping of pets without the landlord's prior permission. If there is a garden are the tenants to be responsible for maintaining it? It would be unrealistic to expect tenants to keep lawns beautifully manicured and to ensure that flowerbeds are planted every year but most tenants would be willing to accept a term that they should not allow a garden to become overgrown. If there is a garden some clause to this effect should be included in the lease.

The forfeiture clause

A forfeiture clause is contained in virtually all professionally drafted leases. Typically it would read like this:

> If any part of the rent is in arrears for more than 21 days whether formally demanded or not or there is any breach of the tenant's obligations under the lease the landlord may re-enter the premises and thereupon the tenancy created by this lease will determine, but without prejudice to any other rights and remedies of the landlord.

What this legalese means is that if a tenant does not behave himself, he will forfeit his rights under the lease. On the face of it, such a clause entitles the landlord to take possession of the premises as soon as the rent is three weeks' in arrears or the tenant commits some other breach. In fact, where the lease is of residential premises, the landlord cannot do this without a court order. However, the clause is still necessary in a lease. If a lease of, say, a year is granted and the tenant fails to pay rent, the landlord would not be entitled to possession until the end of the year. All he could do in the meantime is attempt to sue the tenant for the arrears - not a simple or satisfactory course.

The forfeiture clause has the effect that the landlord has a contractual right to possession. Once he has that right, a court has a power to order possession in his favour if one of the statutory grounds for possession applies. Without that clause, it is impossible for the landlord to recover possession during the term of the lease: with it, recovery will still be far from easy.

The existence of a forfeiture clause does not prevent a lease being an assured shorthold tenancy despite having the effect that a landlord can terminate the lease in less than six months.

From the tenant's perspective

Exempt landlords

Whilst most tenancies are assured and hence give tenants more rights than may be specified in the tenancy agreement, certain landlords are exempt from these provisions altogether. The most significant are local authorities and other government bodies. Council housing is subject to a complete different set of legislation, generally more favourable to tenants, but outside the scope of this book. Where a college grants tenancy to a student attending a course there, it will usually be outside the legislation. Also excluded are holiday lets and lettings which include business or agricultural property.

Agreeing the terms

The terms of a lease are like any other bargain and are a matter for negotiation rather than the diktat of one party. If a prospective tenant believes the landlord is asking too high a rent he should say so. If the landlord refuses to budge on the figure then the tenant must decide whether to pay a higher rent or look for somewhere else.

The landlord's attitude will almost certainly be determined by whether or not he is confident of finding another tenant willing to pay that rent. A tenant may be wary that if he tries to negotiate with the landlord at all, the landlord will simply refuse to grant him the tenancy. That fear may in some circumstances be legitimate. It is unlikely though that anyone who had that attitude would be a particularly pleasant person to have as a landlord. Only a tenant desperate to rent a particular property should allow that sort of fear to dissuade him from polite negotiations.

References

The comments made earlier in this chapter about references from the landlord's point of view should particularly be taken on board by tenants. A person with documents proving he is a desirable character is likely to have a considerable advantage at a meeting with a landlord over others chasing the same property. If a tenant intends giving out anyone's name as a referee, it is sensible and courteous to ask that person's permission in advance.

The effect of the tenancy agreement

Once he signs an agreement a tenant is bound by its terms. If he has agreed to live in a property for a year, then he must assume that he is bound to pay the rent for that year even if he decides to move. Similarly, if he has a beloved cat but signs a lease with a no pets clause then he may not have 'moggy' live with him.

For these reasons a tenant should read thoroughly anything he is asked to sign. If there is something he does not understand, he should have it explained, ideally by a solicitor; failing that by a Citizens' Advice Bureau. It is fair to say that leases on standard forms produced by law stationers are unlikely to contain any unpleasant surprises unless the landlord has added to what appears on the form. Forms produced by landlords or their agents may not be so even-handed.

In some circumstances, a tenant may be granted security of tenure greater than appears to be the case from the lease. For example, if a tenancy was granted before the 28th February 1997 and there was no notice indicating the tenancy was to be an assured shorthold or that the landlord may recover possession for other reasons, it may well be that the tenant is entitled to stay on at the end of the term. If the tenancy is an assured shorthold, it may be possible for the tenant to challenge the level of rent in due course. However, it would not be a good idea to make assumptions based on these possibilities when deciding whether or not to enter into the tenancy agreement.

3

PROVISIONS UNDER THE TENANCY

From the landlord's perspective

Furniture

From a legal point of view it makes very little difference whether or not the landlord provides furniture when letting property. When the original Act of Parliament giving security of tenure was introduced in 1915 furnished tenancies were excluded. However, the legislation has been altered many times since then. The distinction between furnished and unfurnished lettings lost virtually all legal significance after 1977 with the passing of the Rent Act. Despite that a many people still believe that one cannot be a "sitting tenant" if the landlord provides furniture.

The landlord's decision whether or not to furnish the property will depend largely on the sort of tenancy he is granting. Tenants entering into a three year contract are much more likely to be willing to provide their own furniture than tenants renting for only six months. Tenants do not generally expect furniture provided to be of the highest quality.

However, it is essential that any furniture supplied complies with the The Furniture and Furnishings (Fire) (Safety) Regulations. Furniture bought from second hand shops is usually acceptable provided that it too complies with these regulations. If the landlord has previously lived in the property, the furniture he does not want to move to his new home should form the nucleus of what he provides for the tenants.

If he lets a property as furnished, the following would be an absolute minimum of furniture he could provide:
- Sofa and armchair in the living room
- Cabinet or sideboard of some sort
- Kitchen table and chairs
- Cooker
- Refrigerator
- Bed, wardrobe and bedside cabinet in each bedroom

If the property is let to students, a desk and chair should be provided for each student. Large rooms will require more furniture.

The Furniture and Furnishings (Fire) (Safety) Regulations 1988 require landlords to comply with the same regulations appertaining to the provision of fire resistant furniture as those which apply to retailers. All new and secondhand furniture provided in accommodation let for the first time, or replacement furniture in existing let accommodation must comply with the fire resistance requirements (unless it was made before 1950). Under these Regulations the furniture has to:

(i)   have upholstery that complies with the "cigarette test". (A test carried out to a British Standard specification designed to ensure that furniture will not burst into flames when a cigarette is dropped on it)

(ii)   have a filling that complies with further "ignitability tests"

(iii)   have any permanent covers that comply with the "match test"

Furniture which satisfies these requirements is labelled accordingly. Secondhand shops and auctioneers may not sell furniture that does not comply with these regulations. Many landlords will have to replace furniture in their properties to comply with the regulations.

Tenants generally expect even unfurnished properties to be equipped with carpets, curtains and shelving. Supplying a washing machine and tumble drier will make the property more attractive to tenants (a dish-washer, perhaps even more so) but remember machines do break down, particularly with rough handling tenants may subject them to.

Most tenants prefer to provide, or rent, their own television and video. If the landlord does supply electrical equipment he may disclaim any responsibility for repairing them if they break down, but this should be agreed clearly when the tenancy agreement is made. Sometimes the landlord will provide cutlery, crockery and bed-linen, but in respect of such personal items it would not seem unreasonable to expect all but the most impecunious tenants to supply their own.

Cooking utensils such as saucepans and frying pans are normally provided by the landlord where there is a furnished tenancy. Light bulbs are strictly speaking the landlord's responsibility whether the tenancy is furnished or not. It has been known for tenants to ask landlords to pay for washing up liquid and toilet paper: only the most generous comply!

Services

If the tenancy agreement is such that the landlord is responsible for electricity and gas bills, this will not affect the legal nature of the tenancy. Of course, such an arrangement would not be attractive to most landlords if it could be avoided. The tenants' temptation to use more heating than is necessary, knowing someone else is paying for it, may prove irresistible. However, in properties situated in a block of flats there may be a central boiler in which case the landlord may pay a flat fee service charge for the heating. In that case it is often easier for him to settle the bill for this and reflect the fact in the amount of rent charged for the flat. There are maximum prices the landlord can charge for gas and electricity services. Water and sewerage charges may also be paid by the landlord and charged to the tenant through the rent, though usually if the property is self-contained the tenant will be responsible for such charges.

If the property is a house in multiple occupation the landlord will be responsible for paying council tax. However, a landlord may recover this, indirectly, through including the cost within the rent. In order to avoid doubt, it is best that the tenancy agreement sets out who is responsible for the council tax, water charges and other bills.

Sometimes the landlord will elect to provide the tenant with more personal forms of services, such as cleaning, changing the beds and even cooking meals. These services may effecitvely mean that the tenant is granted a licence rather than a lease. If these services are provided when the tenant lives in the same house as the landlord it will for practical pur-poses not be a tenancy in any case.

If the landlord is employing someone to provide these services as in a hostel, the question as to whether or not there is a tenancy will depend upon whether the tenant has exclusive possession of any property. If the landlord's employee visits the room daily to clean it, then the tenant may not have that degree of exclusivity.

If there is not a tenancy, the tenant's (strictly then, licensee's) rights are considerably eradicated. This is a somewhat grey area of the law and it would be most inadvisable for a landlord to provide services purely in the belief that doing so would prevent there being a tenancy.

Repairs

The landlord's basic repairing obligation in respect of the structure of the premises and the electricity, gas and water supplies has already been set out. In a tenancy running for less than seven years the landlord remains under a duty to carry out these types of repairs even if the tenancy agreement has purported to put the responsibility on the tenants.

This though is strictly speaking the limit of the landlord's repairing duties, unless he has agreed to do more. He is not, for instance, required to keep the property well decorated. Somewhat surprisingly, it has been decided by a court that there is no obligation on a landlord to ensure that the property does not become infested by cockroaches. However, if poor decoration or infestation are a consequence of the landlord's failure to perform his repairing obligations, then he will be liable to make good the damage. A leaking roof often, for instance, results in damage being caused inside the premises. Similarly, if the tenant's belongings are damaged because the landlord did not carry out repairs, the landlord will be liable for this. However, the landlord is not responsible for repairing any damage that has been caused by the tenant.

Although the law is not clear on the point, it is generally accepted that landlords are responsible for maintaining any furniture they provide. Furniture in the strict sense requires little maintenance: usually only when carelessness has damaged it. However appliances such as cookers have the same standing as furniture for this purpose and when they break down it is reasonable for the tenants to expect landlords to be responsible for repairs or replacements.

The landlord is however only liable to carry out repairs to defects he should have known about. The most obvious way for him to learn of them is by reason of the tenant's complaint. but he may find out through his own inspection or someone else telling him, in which case his duty to repair will then arise.

Once the landlord is aware of defects, he must remedy them within a reasonable time. What a reasonable time is will depend on the nature of the defect. Where the fault is a broken pipe or a total electrical failure it will be a matter of hours, if that. Even where it is something less urgent, such as missing roof tiles, there can be little excuse for delaying more than a week or so. Only for major structural works, which inevitably take time to arrange, will the landlord be justified in taking longer. Tenants cannot however complain about the landlord's failure to carry out repairs when they have forgotten to tell him anything was wrong.

Landlords have a right to enter the property to inspect the state of repair upon giving 24 hours' written notice.

Safety of gas and electrical appliances
Following a number of highly publicised deaths as a result of carbon monoxide poisoning from defective gas installations in rented property the Gas Safety (Installation and Use) Regulations 1994 required landlords' compliance by 31 October 1995. Further regulations strengthened the impact of these provisions from 31 October 1996.

The main duty on the landlord is a sensible one: not to install a gas appliance unless it can be used without constituting a danger to any person. As a result of the regulations landlords are required to ensure that every gas appliance in the property is maintained in good order and is checked for safety every year by an approved person. This means a tradesman who is registered with CORGI (Council of Registered Gas Installers). British Gas can carry out the work itself, but its prices will tend to be higher than private contractors.

In addition, the landlord must keep a record of the safety checks in respect of each gas appliance and issue it to the tenants, irrespective of whether it is requested, within 14 days of each annual check. CORGI engineers should prepare a formal certificate of safety. This comes in three parts - one copy is for the landlord, one for the tenant and one is kept by the engineer. The record should state any defects identified and any remedial action that has been taken in respect of that defect. The landlord should keep his proof of inspection.

When a new tenancy is granted the landlord should provide the tenant with a copy of the certificate before the tenant moves in. Any tenant who may be affected by a gas appliance is entitled to inspect the record which relates to it upon giving the landlord reasonable notice. A gas appliance for these purposes is one "designed for use by a consumer of gas for heating, lighting, cooking, or other purposes". This includes boilers and other central heating devices as much as it does fires.

A failure to comply with these regulations which resulted in a gas leak or explosion that caused the death of a tenant could lead to the landlord being prosecuted for manslaughter.

As to electrical appliances and electrical systems the landlord should ensure that those supplied such as cooker, microwave, fridge, washing machine, dishwasher, immersion heater, kettle and toaster etc., are safe to use. Where property is in multiple occupation, perhaps where a number of bedsits in the same house have been let, fire regulations apply.

At the end of the tenancy

The lease will normally have spelt out the obligations of the tenants at the end of the term. Under a fairly typical draft tenancy the tenant has to:

- have kept the interior clean and tidy and in a good state of repair and decoration
- have not caused any damage
- have replaced anything they have broken
- replace or pay for repair or replacement of anything damaged
- pay for the laundering of linen (if supplied)
- pay for the laundering of any curtains, blankets or similar items that have been soiled
- put anything they have moved back to its original position

Sometimes leases include a landlord's right to have the premises professionally cleaned at the tenant's expense no matter in what state the property has been left. So long as the tenants have cleaned the property reasonably thoroughly it would seem rather mean to insist on such a right. Likewise if the tenants have washed the sheets themselves, there would seem little point in insisting on them being laundered as well.

Obviously if there is any serious damage, the landlord has every right to demand that this be paid for. However most leases have an exception for fair wear and tear. The odd scratch on the furniture, tear on the wallpaper and even broken plate really falls into this category. The longer the tenancy, the greater the degree of deterioration counting as fair wear and tear.

The landlord will normally be able to recover any loss the tenants' conduct has caused by deducting it from the deposit. Of course, if the tenants have "recovered" the deposit themselves by not paying the final instalment of rent the landlord will not be able to do this. Many tenants, even ones who recover the deposit this way, are fundamentally honest and will pay for any damage if the landlord can persuade them that he has a fair claim. Nothing will deter tenants from acting honourably in this situation more quickly than the landlord demanding sums of money that are unrealistically high in relation to the damage. Theoretically, if the tenants do not pay up, the landlord can try to sue them. In practice, this course is hardly ever worthwhile.

From the tenant's perspective

Furniture and services

Usually tenants will not get a choice about whether or not furniture or services are supplied. It is obviously pointless for someone to apply to rent an unfurnished flat if he does not have any furniture and is not willing to buy some. If furniture is provided by the landlord and the flat is attractive enough it may still be worthwhile taking the tenancy. Furniture does not usually result in the rent being increased greatly. If there is storage space such as a loft or a cellar the landlord's furniture can be hidden away, though it would be a good idea to seek the his permission first.

In normal tenancies, services such as cleaning and the changing of bed linen are not provided. If the tenant is living in a hostel he is far more likely to receive them. Frequently the provision of such services has the effect that he is not granted a tenancy at all. In a hostel, that probably makes very little practical difference to the tenant.

Repairs

If a landlord does not carry out repairs, the tenant has a right to deduct from the rent the costs of having them done. If the tenant adopts such a course, he should keep receipts for all the monies spent. Alternatively, he could continue to pay the rent and sue the landlord for the cost of repairs. Such a course would have little to commend it.

Suing anyone is time-consuming, stressful and often very expensive. It is much better to put the defaulting landlord in a position where if anyone sues it must be him. Of course, if the tenancy is such that the

landlord is entitled to end it and the tenant ceases to pay rent for whatever reason, the landlord may well try to get rid of the tenant. He will
however have to obtain a court order before he can force the tenant to
leave. If the repairs are major and the tenant does not want to pay for
them himself, it is also possible to obtain a court order requiring the
landlord to effect them.

If the landlord is in breach of his repairing obligations for an unreasonable length of time, the tenant may become entitled to damages over
and above the cost of repairs. These will be to compensate him for the
unpleasantness of living in a home in a serious state of disrepair.
Obviously, the amount awarded will depend on the extent of disrepair
and the length of time it persists after the landlord had become aware of
it. A damp patch on a bedroom wall for a few months might be worth
only £100, whereas awards well over £5,000 have been made where
there has been a failure to provide heating or hot water over several
years. The amount of rent the tenant pays may also have a bearing on the
amount of damages: the higher the rent, the higher the damages.

In some circumstances, a local authority will be prepared to intervene
to compel a landlord to carry out repairs. The local environmental health
officer can advise on whether he considers it appropriate for the authority to become involved.

With common sense and co-operation, neither landlord nor tenant
should need to have recourse to these legal rules. When tenants move
into premises landlords are often prepared to pay for materials to enable
them to redecorate so long as tenants are willing to carry out the work
themselves. This seems a sensible arrangement from both sides. The
landlord gets his property redecorated cheaply; the tenants get to choose
the decor they have to live with. Understandably, some landlords are not
so enthusiastic about this arrangement if the tenants show a preference
for extreme or outrageous colours: a colour scheme not so distinctive
that it might deter future tenants is a reasonable requirement!

Whatever the strict legal position, if essential electrical items such as
a cooker or a fridge break down, most landlords are willing to pay for
their repair or replacement. If the landlord asks the tenant to arrange such
repairs or replacement himself, the tenant should co-operate. Particularly
for replacements, a maximum price should be agreed in advance.
Normally the best way for the landlord to repay the tenant is to simply

accept a reduced rent for the next instalment or however long it takes to cover the cost. If the rent is being paid by standing order, the landlord can simply reimburse the tenant by paying the money to him.

Council Tax, Water and other bills

A tenant will normally be responsible for paying Council Tax. An exception to this is if the property is in multiple occupation whereby it will become the landlord's responsibility.

If the accommodation is self-contained water and sewerage charges will also become the tenant's responsibility. Sometimes however, a landlord will pay the water and sewerage charge himself and then include the cost of this within the rent.

If there is any doubt as to who should pay the council tax the local authority should provide guidance. As to who should pay other bills, for example gas, electricity and telephone these can be agreed with the landlord; although it is usual for the the tenant to pay for them.

4

FINDING A TENANT OR A LANDLORD

From the landlord's perspective

Agents

Perhaps the most fundamental thing a landlord needs to decide is whether to use an agent, both to find tenants and subsequently manage the premises. The advantages of using an agent are obvious: they "know the ropes" and are likely to have tenants on their books already. Some, but not all, will check references. They should be able to give advice on a realistic level of rent. They will draw up the tenancy agreement and should be able to do it in such a way as to avoid the disaster of giving the tenant a permanent right to stay in the property.

Lanlords should only consider using an agent who is either a member of the National Approved Letting Scheme (NALS) or belongs to one of the professional bodies that supports it, i.e. the Royal Institution of Chartered Surveyors (RICS), the Association of Residential Letting Agents (ARLA), the Incorporated Society of Valuers and Auctioneers, and the National Association of Estate Agents (NAEA). These bodies ensure that the agents operate to each organisation's standards and code of practice. NALS require certain minimum service standards to be met by members. Members must:-

- · already be a member of RICS, ARLA or NAEA
- · operate an internal complaints procedure
- · maintain professional indemnity insurance (to cover against the possibility of legal actions against them)
- · control a client's money protection scheme (so that a landlord or tenant will get his money back if it is lost or misappropriated by the agent).
- · be linked to a legally binding arbitration service.

In addition, the organisations may be a useful source to turn to in the event of the landlord having a grievance with the agent. (Each of the organisations should provide details of members in your area Telephone numbers are: NALS: 01926 496683, RICS: 0870 3331 600, ARLA 01923 896555, and NAEA: 01926 410785).

Some agencies offer a guaranteed income even if the tenant defaults on the rent. Agencies who make offers of this sort should immediately arouse suspicions. It may not prove any easier to enforce such a promise than it is to enforce the tenant's promise to pay rent. If the promise is made in the name of a limited company, it will only be enforceable against the company, which will often turn out to have no assets. The owner of the company will not be personally liable.

Some agencies insist on rent being paid by the tenant to them rather than directly to the landlord. Agencies have a legitimate interest in protecting their fees and cannot entirely be blamed for this. However, if an agency gets into financial difficulties there is a danger that a landlord may find himself losing rent held by the agent. It would be inadvisable to agree to such an arrangement with any but the longest established companies.

Landlords sometimes use solicitors to draw up tenancy agreements for them. This should not be necessary, but mistakes can be made both by landlords acting for themselves and agents. Instructing a solicitor to do the work should be safer, though even solicitors can make mistakes. Any adviser, whether an agent or solicitor, who makes a costly mistake in drawing up a tenancy agreement will be liable to make up the loss suffered by the landlord. In practice, enforcing such a claim is never easy. The landlord should double check that his advisers have done everything necessary before putting his signature to the tenancy agreement or allowing the tenant start living at the premises.

If agents are appointed to manage the property, it should be agreed in writing what exactly constitutes management. The following are matters that agents often look after:

· transferring utility bills and council tax into the name of the tenant
· arrangement of repairs
· paying for repairs (agents will normally only agree to do

this if the rent is being paid directly to them and they are authorised to deduct these costs from it)
· replacing any item, such as a fridge, which is beyond repair
· chasing tenants if they fall into rent arrears
· serving notices of intention to seek possession if the landlord instructs them to do so (agents should not commence court proceedings except through a solicitor)
· visiting the property at regular intervals (the frequency of which should be specified) to check that the tenants are not causing any damage
· dealing with any complaints that may be made by, for instance, neighbours
· banking the rental receipts if the landlord is abroad
· should it prove necessary, dealing with the council's housing benefit department

The agent's management fee might be 10-15% of the rent. If agents arrange repairs, it is unlikely they will negotiate to get the best deal from tradesmen the way a property owner paying with his own money might.

It is illegal for agencies to charge tenants for merely giving out the address of landlords. It is a criminal offence under the Accommodation Agencies Act 1953, although very few prosecutions are brought. Most agents in any case charge the landlord rather than the tenant.

Fees vary and it is worth shopping around. For finding tenants 10% of the rent charged over the term of the tenancy would be fairly typical. Thus if the tenancy were for six months at a rent of £300 per month the fee would be 10% of £1,800: £180.

Some agents, rather than charging a percentage of the total rent, charge say three weeks' or a month's rent. This scale for payment is more likely to be attractive to a landlord letting a property for a long term. Sometimes extra charges are made for providing the written lease and for checking references. A management service is likely incur an extra 5%. Some agents include a clause in their terms that if a tenant they have introduced subsequently buys the property then they are entitled to the same interest as estate agents who might have sold the property, i.e. perhaps 2% of the purchase price.

An agent should view the premises so that he can fairly describe it to any interested tenants, but some merely take details from the landlord. Some agents are prepared to show the property to prospective tenants if the landlord wants them to do so, others will merely arrange appointments for the landlord to do this.

A landlord considering instructing an agent should check whether the agent intends to advertise the property or merely wait for prospective tenants to walk through his door. If the agent has offices on a busy street which make it clear he is a lettings agent, the latter will be a perfectly good way of attracting customers, though the saving in advertising costs should be reflected in the agent's prices.

Advertisements

The classified ads column of local newspapers are usually a good means of attracting tenants. Such papers will read by most people seeking a property to rent in that area and the charges are fairly small - a three line advert in a local newspaper around London would at the time of writing be around £6, elsewhere slightly less. The London Evening Standard is considerably more expensive - about £25 for the same advert, but extremely effective for property reasonably close to central London. National newspapers also carry such adverts in regionally distributed sections. The Guardian, for instance, currently only charges £6 for a three line advert covering the London area.

LOOT, (0207 328 1771) a newspaper that consists solely of adverts which can be placed free over the phone or in writing, is distributed throughout London and the Home Counties. It contains a substantial property section, is published daily and currently costs £1.10.

Free ad papers now also exist in several major British cities and local radio stations may be prepared to provide information about available lettings. Often tenants can be found simply by placing a card in a shop window. Most colleges and universities keep lists of accommodation available to students and will be pleased to include any new property without charge. Many college/university accommodation offices will be able to provide information about realistic rent levels, although their primary interest should be in helping students rather than landlords.

Of course, the internet has, as for most things, brought further opportunities. There are many websites that are available where one can advertise letting property. Any fairly good search engine should provide several website addresses. The difficulty in using the internet, though, is the fact that whilst there is a large amount of potential, there are only a limited number of internet users who live or want to live in the locality where you are advertising.

Where rates are by the line, abbreviations are the order of the day. The following is a real advert from the Evening Standard:

> *SW13 beaut res area grd flr dbl bdrm lg gch bth/shwr rm small k wm ideal prof cple.*

Although this was more decipherable than many, what "wm" means is a complete mystery. Most prospective tenants would have no idea what it is. Such a detailed description - abbreviated or otherwise - is in any case fairly pointless. People want to know the area, size and price. If these meet their criteria they will ring up and find out more details. Here is another advert from the same edition but this one was probably just as effective although a quarter of the length and price:

> *N16 1 bd unfurn £110 pw*

Some papers now refuse to accept abbreviations at all.

Going back to Mrs Healey and her flat, she might reasonable advertise it as:

> *E15 4 bedroom flat, lounge, close tube, shops, separate bath and toilet £320 per week, tel 0208 123 4567*

Abbreviated to appear in the Evening Standard, this would read:

> *E15 4b/r, 1l/r, close LT, sep btr w.c. £320 pw 0208 123 4567*

Local authorities and housing associations

Some local authorities also take tenancies of privately owned properties. These are then let to individuals whom the council is under a duty to house. The local authority usually requires a tenancy of at least two years. In return, it will guarantee the rent throughout the period and carry out repairs and redecoration at the end of the term.

Some authorities now carry out letting of this sort through housing associations. In London authorities now sometimes even take properties on this basis in neighbouring boroughs as well as within their own boundaries. People occupying properties sub-let by local authorities often have particular problems. A landlord prepared to let in this way may therefore feel that doing so is socially responsible and desirable. The starting point for letting to a local authority would be to phone the housing department of the council in question.

Showing the property

Once the landlord has received a response to his advertisement, the next stage is to make arrangements for people to view the property. If he is not living there himself and has to make a special visit to the property, there is no reason why he should not make all the appointments on the same day. He should try to keep appointments a reasonable distance of time apart. It is not in anyone's interests to have more than one group of people looking at a property at the same time.

Prospective tenants tend to be a lot more reliable about turning up on time than people who are considering buying a property. If either party has to cancel an appointment, then it is common courtesy to do all one can to let the other party know. This cannot be emphasised too much when someone has to make a special journey for that appointment.

If tenants like the property and the landlord likes the tenants, there is obviously no reason why it should not be let there and then. This is much easier to accomplish if the landlord has already prepared a draft agreement and any notices relevant to the tenancy. It is vital for the landlord to remember to hand over and obtain a receipt for the notices before signing the tenancy agreement or accepting any money.

Unless the landlord is completely convinced of the tenants' respectability, accepting a cheque at this stage may be risky. Certainly, the keys should not be handed over until the cheque has cleared. If it bounces before the tenants move in, there is still a tenancy agreement and although the legal position is not entirely clear, the tenants may be entitled to live there. It is always best err on the side of caution and wait a couple of days. A tenancy is a commitment by both parties and it may be useful to have a short period of reflection.

From the tenant's perspective

Advertisements, agents and viewing

The sources of advertisements people might use when looking for a property are of course the same as those used by landlords. Prospective tenants sometimes try advertising their own needs. Although this may not be a particularly reliable way of finding a home, there is always a possibility that a landlord will see the advertisement and respond to it rather than placing his own advert. Placing such an advert in a free ads paper or a local newspaper, where the fee for a couple of lines is unlikely to be more than a few pounds, is a reasonable investment.

Beware of any agent who asks for a fee in advance or indeed who intends to charge tenants at all. Often estate agents who do not advertise the fact that they deal with lettings can help in finding rented property. Even if they do not have anything suitable on their own books they are likely to know of other local agents who do.

When viewing property prospective tenants should come armed with documents that prove their respectability and sufficient cash to pay the first month's rent and any reasonable deposit the landlord may ask for. If a property is in heavy demand, "first come, first served" is likely to apply and being there with everything the landlord is likely to require is the best way of getting to the head of the queue. Even if the property is not in such heavy demand, by doing this you will show the landlord that you are organised and respectable and you will make a good impression.

5

THE RENT

From the landlord's perspective

Payment of Rent

The landlord and tenant should agree before the lease is completed on how the rent is to be paid. Some landlords like to physically collect the rent. This gives them an opportunity to visit the premises regularly and check that all is well. Doing this can be quite an effective method of ensuring that the tenant pays on time. It is much easier to "forget" to put money in the post than to find an excuse not to hand it over when actually faced with the landlord.

Probably the most reliable method of ensuring the tenant complies with his obligations is to have him complete a standing order. This is an instruction to his bank to pay regularly a certain amount of money into the landlord's bank account. A form on which this can be done will be provided by most banks though landlords can draw up their own. The account out of which the tenant pays the rent will have to be a current account. Most deposit accounts do not have any facility for standing orders. Bank account numbers and sort codes are set out on cheque books and statements.

Mrs Healey prepared such a form in anticipation of finding a suitable tenant. She wrote in the details of her own bank account and left the tenants' details to be completed when she found someone to whom she wanted to let the property:

> To the Manager,
> [Name and address of tenant's bank],
>
> Please pay £320 every Monday from my account held at your branch, no. [number of tenant's account] to the credit of account no. 03 67 89 12345678 held in the name

of Mrs A H Healey, at Barclay's Bank, 55 High Road,
St Albans, Herts (sort code 03 67 89).

Signed .... tenant

The landlord should have the tenant complete and sign the form. It is
then advisable for the landlord to send it to the tenant's bank rather than
relying on the tenant to do so himself. (Direct debits which are similar
to, and often confused with, standing orders are not appropriate for use
by private landlords. They enable one person to take money directly out
of another's bank account. The banks understandably restrict the right to
do this to large organisations.)

If the landlord does want to collect his rent by standing order, it is
advisable to have the tenant complete the standing order form when the
lease is signed and perhaps even to stipulate in the lease that the rent is
to be paid in this way. As with any other term of a lease, it becomes
much harder for a landlord to insist upon payment in this way once the
tenant is installed in the property.

Raising the rent: assured and assured shorthold tenancies

If a tenancy is granted for a specific term, the rent will remain the
same throughout that term unless the lease has specified circumstances
in which it can be increased or the tenant agrees. Once that term has
expired the landlord can try to set a new rent. If the tenancy is a weekly
or monthly one, the landlord cannot attempt to increase the rent until
after the tenancy has run for at least a year.

There are also procedural restrictions on the landlord's ability to
increase the rent. The landlord must serve a notice of increase. This must
give the tenant at least one month's warning of the increase. If rent is
paid quarterly then three months' notice has to be given; if yearly, six
months' notice.

The notice must be on an official form called "Landlord's notice
proposing a new rent under an Assured Periodic Tenancy or Agricultural
Occupancy". This form can be obtained from a law stationers or rent
assessment panel.

If there is more than one tenant, it must be addressed to all of them. If
the landlord wants to alter any other terms of the tenancy, perhaps

converting an unfurnished tenancy into a furnished one then he must also serve a notice. This is similar to the one in respect of a rent increase and likewise gives the tenants an opportunity to accept or reject the change.

The tenant on receiving a notice of increase, if he does not agree with the proposal, can apply to a Rent Assessment Committee (see below) to determine what the rent should be. There is, naturally, the option for the tenant to try to persuade the landlord not to impose the increase, but if an impasse occurs - unless the tenant does apply to the rent assessment committee - the rent increase as proposed in the formal notice will occur through default.

In practice many - perhaps most - landlords simply ignore the notice requirement and tell the tenant informally that they are increasing the rent. So long as there is a reasonably amicable relationship between the landlord and the tenant there is little to be gained by complying with the legal formalities. However, if the landlord and tenant subsequently have a falling out it is the landlord who will suffer problems. Unless there has been some sort of formal agreement to increase the rent, the tenant cannot be compelled to pay the increased rent.

The same rules which apply to shorthold tenancies concerning initial rents and increasing them apply to assured tenancies. However, with an assured shorthold tenancy the tenant has a right to apply to a rent assessment committee to alter the rent agreed between him and the landlord at the beginning of the letting. If the tenancy began on or after 28 February 1997 a tenant may apply only once within the first six months. If more than six months have elapsed no application can be made.

The circumstances in which the committee can interfere with the rent are very limited. It will only do so if it believes that the landlord is charging a rent significantly higher than the landlord might have been expected to obtain having regard to the level of rents charged for similar properties in the same location. Such an application is made by the tenant obtaining and sending to the committee a prescribed form, blank copies of which can be obtained from law stationers or rent officers.

Rent Assessment Committee

Any application to a Rent Assessment Committee must be done before the date on which the new rent falls due, otherwise the committee has no power to consider the rent. The rent will be based on what a reasonable market rent for the property would be. If there is a scarcity of rented property in the area, that will be taken into account. What the rent assessment committee will not do is allow a landlord to charge an exorbitant rent to a tenant who is desperate to carry on living in the same home when no-one else would be willing to pay such a high price.

When an application is made to a Rent Assessment Committee it will usually arrange for its members - normally there are three of them (one of whom is a lawyer, one a property valuer and one a layman) - to inspect the property. They will then have an informal hearing where the landlord and tenant can advance any arguments about the proper level of rent. It is possible for the committee to make their decision on consideration of the relevant papers if the landlord or tenant does not request a hearing.

Generally, the committee will decide what rent could be reasonably expected if the property were let on the open market under a tenancy on identical terms. Neither increases in the value of the letting through voluntary improvements by the tenant, nor reductions in value, which have occurred through the tenant's failure to keep the property in a respectable manner, will be considerations for the committee.

After their considerations, the committee may either agree the rent proposed or set a different one (it can be a higher or lower rent). The amount of rent that the committee finally decides upon is usually back-dated to the date of expiry of the notice. However, if the tenant can show he is being caused "undue hardship" the committee can use its discretion to delay the increase until any date up to the date of assessment.

If a rent is set using this procedure, the landlord cannot attempt to raise it again for a year. However if the term of the tenancy expires he may obtain possession against the tenant. There is nothing to stop a landlord from then granting a new tenancy to someone else at the old rent, assuming of course that he can find anyone willing to pay it.

Raising the rent: tenancies granted before 15 January 1989
Strictly speaking in the case of tenancies granted before 15 January 1989 the landlord has no right to increase the rent except by applying to the rent officer for a fair rent. Fair rents generally are discussed in the tenant's section below. As fair rents are considerably below market rents, the landlord may find that applying for a fair rent will actually result in the rent decreasing.

Even once an increased rent has been assessed, the landlord can only implement it by serving a notice of increase on the tenant. The landlord can ask the tenant to agree to an increased rent without applying to the rent officer. An agreement reached this way will only be binding if it is written and signed by the landlord and the tenant and it contains, amongst other things. a statement that the tenant is entitled to apply for a fair rent. It should also be noted that neither the landlord's nor tenant's right to apply to a rent officer can be excluded either in the lease or by any other prior agreement.

The rent book

If a landlord collects rent, rather than having it paid by standing order, it is a good idea to provide the tenant with a rent book and to sign it every time rent is paid. Where the rent is paid weekly, provision of a rent book is a legal requirement, and certain information must be stated in the book. It is a criminal offence for the landlord not to provide a rent book where the rent is payable weekly. Books in the correct form can be obtained from many general stationers.

From the tenant's perspective

Tenancies granted after 14 January 1989

The landlord's obligation to serve the appropriate notice to an assured tenant before increasing the rent is discussed earlier. If the landlord tries to increase the rent without serving a notice, the tenant must decide whether pay it. If the increase is an unreasonable one, particularly if it is to a level which means the tenant would rather quit the property than pay, the tenant should simply carry on paying the old rent.

If on the other hand the increase is reasonable, perhaps equivalent to no more than the rate of inflation, there is probably little to be gained by refusing to pay it. Doing so will only be likely to antagonise the landlord. If he is entitled to, the landlord may well apply for a possession order. It is easy enough for him to serve a proper notice of increase.

A tenant who pays an increase when the landlord has not gone through the proper procedure may eventually be able to get the money back. This rather devious course would not have been available had the tenant taken advantage of the landlord's failure straight away: he would merely have driven the landlord into following the correct procedure.

Tenancies granted before 15 January 1989

In the case of tenancies granted before 15 January 1989, including those that have subsequently been renewed, the tenant has considerably greater rights to apply for a registered rent. This right is much more draconian than those discussed earlier in relation to assured and assured shortholds.

The application is made to a rent officer rather than a Rent Assessment Committee and is made on the official form which can be obtained from the rent officer. This asks about the property and also requires the tenant to specify what he thinks the fair rent should be. Specifying a sum considerably less than the present rent is probably the best course. Once the application is made, the rent officer will send a form asking the landlord to provide certain information. The rent officer then inspects the premises and will, if either party has requested it, arrange a meeting between himself the landlord and the tenant. He will then decide upon the rent to be registered. The landlord and the tenant both have a right of appeal to a rent assessment committee if dissatisfied with his decision.

The landlord cannot compel the tenant to agree to any increase in rent without the rent first being referred to a rent officer. In the case of these particular tenancies the tenant is usually in a very strong position to resist any increase unless there is already a fair rent. Once a fair rent is assessed the landlord is not entitled to recover any more rent than that assessed. In the unlikely event of the fair rent being more than is currently paid, the landlord is not immediately entitled to increase the rent. He can only do so once the term of the contract has expired.

> *To give an example of this:* Suppose 41c Wilson Road, a much smaller flat, has been let since 1 July 1987 by Mrs Healey to Mr Foot. This has been renewed every year. The rent payable from 1 July 1994 was £200 per week. Mr Foot applies for a registered rent and one is determined on 31 March 1995 at £175 per week. From 1 April onwards Mr Foot will only have to pay that amount. On the other hand had the rent been raised to £210 per week, Mrs Healey could only charge £200 per week until the expiry of the lease on 30 June 1995. Then she could recover the higher

rent but would first have to serve a notice of increase. Mr Foot would be entitled to leave the premises if he did not wish to pay the higher rent. In any case Mrs Healey is entitled to agree to take a lower rent. However even if he enters into another agreement to pay a rent higher than that registered Mr Foot could not be compelled to pay it. Indeed if he pays a higher rent, he is entitled to sue to recover it for two years after he has paid it.

Registered rents are almost always less than the rent agreed between the landlord and the tenant. There is no specific formula used by rent officers, but they have to disregard any increase of value caused by a scarcity of rented property in the vicinity.

The best way to find out what a registered rent on a particular property is likely to be is to examine the register kept by the rent officer. From this it will be possible to compare rents recently set on similar properties. It is important to remember to check the date on any assessment. An assessment made several years ago will have little relevance to a new application.

6

TAX AND HOUSING BENEFIT

From the landlord's perspective - tax
The rent received by a landlord is treated as his income for tax purposes.The basis upon which it is treated depends to an extent upon whether the property let is furnished or unfurnished. There are some differences in the way that furnished and unfurnished premises are taxed but these are unlikely to have any practical effect on the small landlord. If the landlord provides meals and services for a number of tenants, the resulting income may be treated as coming from a trade rather than property. Again, this will not have a great practical impact on the amount of tax payable, but the landlord may be able to persuade the Revenue to allow him a greater range of deductions from his income.

Payment directly to the Inland Revenue
An agent who receives tax can be required by the Inland Revenue to pay a proportion to the Revenue rather than to the landlord on account of the landlord's tax liability. A direction is likely to be made where the landlord has previously defaulted on payments. An agent who does not comply with such a direction can be personally liable for the lost tax as well as having to pay a fine. If the landlord lives abroad the tenant, is under an obligation to deduct basic rate income tax from the rent and pay it directly to the Inland Revenue.

Exemptions from tax
Where the landlord lets rooms in his own home a certain amount of rent - currently £4,250 per year- is exempt from taxation. The allowance can be shared or allocated to one of them if there is more than one landlord. However the landlord(s) will not be able to deduct any expenses on the £4,250 itself nor any surplus subject to tax. Where a person obtains an income substantially in excess of this amount from renting rooms at his home he should seek an accountant's advice as to whether or not it is in his interests to claim the allowance.

Deductions from tax

Expenditure on the property may be deducted from the rental income to reach a taxable figure. The following are all accepted by the Inland Revenue as being proper matters for deduction:

> *insuring the property*
> *repairs and maintenance*
> *agents' fees or commission*
> *water rates*
> *council tax*
> *rent paid to a superior landlord (most usually ground rent and/or service charges payable under a long lease)*
> *legal fees*
> *interest paid on loans secured on the property, i.e. mortgages (but there are exceptions to this entitlement)*

Improvements, rather than repairs, carried out on the property are not deductible. In practice the Revenue is unlikely to enquire closely about the nature of work carried out unless an enormous allowance is claimed.

Stamp duty

Stamp duty is payable on leases. For furnished tenancies lasting less than a year this is merely a nominal sum of £1. Otherwise, normally it is 1% of the annual rent. There is however strictly speaking no obligation to pay this duty. The only sanction for non-payment is that a court should refuse to receive an unstamped document in evidence. If a dispute arises, which looks likely to lead to court proceedings, the landlord should consider stamping the document. A penalty may be levied for late payment, but the fear of this is not generally enough to encourage landlords of short-term tenancies to pay it in advance. In practice, courts frequently overlook the rule about not looking at unstamped leases.

From the landlord's perspective (housing benefit)
Payment direct to the landlord

Housing benefit is essentially a payment made to the tenant rather than the landlord. However, local authorities are under a duty to prevent its abuse. It is therefore possible to arrange for the local authority paying the benefit to do so directly to the landlord. The local authority must agree to do this where there are eight weeks' arrears of rents, unless it would be in the interests of the tenant not to do this.

Where any claimant has rent arrears either of £200 or arrears for more than six weeks the landlord can request direct payments without the need for the tenant's consent. Since 2 January 1996 it has been possible to make an application for determination of housing benefit before the tenancy in order to determine how much of a proposed rent is eligible for housing benefit. An application is made direct to the housing authority who then pass the application on to a rent officer for determination.

Housing benefit and possession for arrears of rent

If a landlord has let a property knowing that the tenant is going to claim housing benefit, then it is probably best for him to wait while the local authority sorts matters out. If the arrears are accruing through no fault of the tenant's, it is unlikely that the court would exercise any discretion in the landlord's favour. Once there are two months' arrears of rent and Ground 8 applies the court has to order possession regardless of any fault by the housing benefit authorities.

If on the other hand the tenant had taken on a tenancy on the implicit understanding that he was going to pay the rent himself but then immediately applies for housing benefit, the court is more likely to sympathise with the landlord. An intermediate situation might be the case of a longstanding tenant who has paid his rent reliably but who needs to apply for housing benefit because he has lost his job.

From the tenant's perspective (tax)

Direct payment of rent to the Inland Revenue

If the landlord lives abroad the tenant is obliged to pay a proportion of the rent directly to the Inland Revenue and tenants should contact the local tax office as soon as they move in to establish the position in relation to this. A landlord who envisaged being paid the full amount directly is unlikely to be very pleased by the tenants paying his tax for him. There is in practice very little that can be done about this. If the tenants do not co-operate with the Inland Revenue they may well find themselves personally liable to pay the landlord's tax!

From the tenant's perspective (housing benefit)

Housing benefit is a State payment to tenants on low incomes to assist them with their rent payments.Those in receipt of income support should receive the entire amount of the rent. Students are in almost all cases disqualified from receiving housing benefit. Tenants should be aware that housing benefit is now paid four weeks in arrears. This produces more hurdles for potential tenants in need of benefit since a claimant will have to find sufficient funds to pay the rent before moving in. In most private landlord and tenant relationships advance rent is almost always a pre-requisite to moving in.

Backdated claims

Tenants are entitled to claim housing benefit back-dated to one year from the date they made the claim but the tenant must show good cause for not having made the claim earlier. This is interpreted liberally by many authorities and a simple non-awareness of entitlement will often be sufficient.

Excessive rent

If the local authority believes the rent is excessive for the type of property or where the property is grander than the tenant reasonably needs, it may reduce the amount of housing benefit it pays to what it considers an appropriate amount. If a fair rent or registered rent has been assessed in respect of the property, the local authority will not pay a greater amount than that. The authority cannot exercise this power on the basis of the accommodation being more than the tenant reasonably needs during the first three months the tenant claims if he had previously been paying the rent himself.

There is in turn an exception to that exception if the tenant had been eligible for housing benefit in the previous 12 months. There are restrictions on exercising the power where the tenant is a pensioner, unable to work through illness or has children under 18. If housing benefit is reduced under this power, the reduction will be equivalent to the proportion by which the local authority believes too much rent is being paid.

Suppose a tenant is paying £100 per week in rent, but the local authority only believes it should be £75. The tenant's income is such that he is entitled to have half his rent paid by the housing benefit authorities. With the deduction he would have £37.50 paid rather than £50. (As the difference between £100 and £75 is 25%, the 25% is deducted from £50)

Housing benefit is only intended to cover the rent itself and not ancillary matters which may be included in the payment described as rent. Therefore if the landlord pays the water rates, provides heating, pays the utility bills, provides services or meals, the amount of housing benefit will be adjusted to deduct these. However, if the landlord waives rent for up to eight weeks because the tenant has carried out repairs or redecoration, housing benefit will still be paid during that period.

Payment of housing benefit

Housing benefit should be paid within 14 days of the authority receiving a valid claim. In practice it often takes a lot longer to process applications. A tenant finding himself in a position where the landlord is threatening legal action because of arrears which have built up due to non-payment of housing benefit should instruct a solicitor who will then put pressure on the local authority to pay the arrears.

There is no legal obligation on a tenant who receives housing benefit to hand it over to his landlord. Of course, if he does not do so the landlord can sue him, but it will be arrears of rent that he is sued for not the housing benefit. A criminal prosecution alleging theft against a tenant who retained housing benefit failed for this reason some years ago.

7

TRANSFERRING A TENANCY

From the landlord's perspective

Transfers to a new tenant

Generally speaking residential tenancies whenever granted cannot be transferred from one tenant to another unless the landlord agrees. If the tenant moves out and purports to transfer the tenancy to another person, the landlord should have no difficulty in obtaining a possession order. The new occupant will not be a protected, statutory or assured tenant and hence will have no statutory protection.

Where a tenancy was granted after 14 January 1989 and the landlord had charged a premium, then this rule does not apply unless the agreement contained a term which specifically prohibits subletting or assigning the tenancy. A premium can include for instance any payment towards the landlord's costs of preparing the tenancy agreement and a deposit in excess of two months' rent. If the landlord appointed an agent to let the property and some or all of the agent's fees were paid by the tenant, this can constitute a premium.

Death of the landlord

Generally speaking the death of the landlord has less effect on the tenancy than that of the tenant. The tenancy continues. However, most of the rights that the landlord had will pass to his estate. These rights will be exercised by his personal representatives, also known as executors (if he made a will) and his administrators (if he did not). These are the people with responsibility for sorting out the landlord's affairs. They are not necessarily the same people who will actually be entitled to the landlord's property, who are beneficiaries. Often the personal representatives are professional advisers such as solicitors or a bank. They however have to act in the best interests of the beneficiaries.

Once the lease has vested in personal representatives they are entitled to do anything that the deceased landlord could have done, thus they are able to sue for arrears of rent and breaches of covenant of the original lease; even if such breaches occurred before the landlord's death.

It sometimes happens that tenants who have been allowed by a landlord to stay in premises very cheaply as a gesture of friendship, find themselves facing far less generous executors. Where personal representatives do act in a way that was very different from the landlord, it may be possible to make an application to the court in respect of the landlord's estate. This involves a complicated area of law outside the scope of this book and is certainly not the sort of action that can be contemplated without the help of a solicitor.

If the tenancy is an assured shorthold, the personal representatives and anyone to whom they pass the property whether it goes to a beneficiary or it is sold, will be able rely on the notice to evict the tenants. If a notice had been served before the death of the landlord saying that the landlord could recover possession because he had lived there himself and the tenancy began on or after 15 January 1989, then this would have the same wide effect after the landlord's death. On the other hand if the notice had said that the landlord intended living there some time in the future or the tenancy began before that date, it cannot be relied upon if the property is sold by the personal representatives.

If there are other grounds for possession, such as arrears of rent, executors or anyone else to whom the property passes are in exactly the same position as the original landlord.

Where the tenant had been sharing accommodation with the landlord and hence had no statutory protection, then the position is legally complicated. In the majority of cases the tenant will only get the benefit of statutory protection if no action has been taken by the personal representatives within two years of the landlord's death.

From the tenant's perspective

The position when the tenant dies is complicated to say the least. Often tenancies are granted jointly to two people. In that case the survivor of them will be entitled to stay on as the sole tenant. There are intricate statutory rules to decide when and if another person who was previously not a tenant, is entitled to succeed on the death of a tenant. Different rules apply depending upon whether or not the tenancy was granted before or after 15 January 1989.

Death of the tenant: tenancy granted before 15 January 1989
Where the tenancy was originally granted before 15 January 1989 the following rules apply:

· *the surviving spouse of a tenant has an automatic right to carry on living there regardless of whether or not the tenancy was in joint names. This right however only applies so long as the spouse was living at the property at the time of the former tenant's death ("spouse" includes a person who was living with the tenant as his or her husband or wife even if not legally married. Homosexual partners have also recently become included into this category)*
· *where the tenant died without leaving a spouse any other member of the tenant's family who had lived with him at the property for at least two years up to his death is entitled to succeed ("members of the family" includes children and grandchildren - whether natural, step- or adopted - parents and brothers and sisters. Platonic adult friends will not be treated as "members of the family")*
· *if there is more than one family member living with the tenant at the time of his death, they can agree which is to become the tenant. If they cannot agree, they can apply to the court for a decision as to which has the best entitlement.*
· *where the surviving spouse has succeeded to the tenancy, the new tenancy will be treated as if it had been granted before 15 January 1989 except that succession will only be possible by someone who had been living at the property with both the original tenant and the successor for the two years up to their respective deaths.*
· *where a member of the family other than the spouse succeeds he will only become an assured tenant and the resulting tenancy will be treated like any other granted after 14 January 1989 but without any right to a further succession.*
· *only two successions are permitted*

To give an example: Mr and Mrs Watson had been granted a joint tenancy in 1978. Mr Watson died in 1983. In 1985 Mrs Watson then met a Mr Fowler. In that year he and his, then 13 year old, daughter, Linda Fowler, moved into the property, where he co-habited with Mrs Watson. Mrs Watson died in 1990. Mr Fowler died in 1992. Linda, who had continued living in the property married in 1993. In 1994 Linda died. Is her husband entitled to the tenancy?

The first issue is, do the pre-1989 rules apply? The answer to that is yes: it is the date of the original tenancy not of any subsequent succession that is crucial. Then, was Mrs Watson entitled to succeed Mr Watson? Clearly she was and as they were joint tenants it was not strictly speaking a succession, so she became a tenant in her own right. Then, was Mr Fowler entitled to succeed Mrs Watson? Yes, so long as they had lived together as husband and wife for he would be treated as her spouse. This was the first succession.

Was Linda, then, entitled to succeed Mr Fowler? Probably. She was his daughter and hence a member of his family. She had been living with him at the property for more than two years. Being Mrs Watson's step-daughter she was also a member of her family and had been living with her as such for two years up to her death. The second succession.

There are two reasons why Linda's husband would not be entitled to succeed.

a) only two successions are allowed

b) he had never been a member of the original tenant's - i..e. Mrs Watson's - family. The fact that he had lived in the property less than two years would not of itself prevent him succeeding, although it would have done had he been anyone other than a spouse

Death of the tenant: tenancy granted after 14 January 1989

The only basis on which there can be succession to an assured tenancy is where the tenant's spouse was living with him at the property the time of his death. It does not matter whether or not the tenancy agreement was only signed by the deceased tenant. "Spouse" here again includes a person who was living as husband or wife with the tenant without being legally married; in addition, the House of Lords decided that a homosexual partner also falls within the expression.

There can only be one succession under these rules. Therefore if a person dies and is succeeded to the tenancy by his wife and she remarries, the new husband will never be entitled to succeed. However if the tenancy had originally been granted jointly to the husband and wife there will not be a succession when the wife becomes the sole tenant on the husband's death. The new husband would be entitled to succeed, but would not be able in turn to pass the tenancy onto any new wife.

Bankruptcy

If the tenant himself goes bankrupt it is unlikely to have much effect on the tenancy. The tenancy is unlikely to be an asset of much interest to his creditors. When a person goes bankrupt leases he owns vests in his trustee-in-bankruptcy. If the tenancy involves the payment of a very substantial rent it is possible that the trustee might disclaim it, which would entitle the landlord to immediate possession. If the term of the tenancy has expired, there will be a statutory tenancy and this will not vest in the trustee. A bankrupt tenant may be able to get housing benefit.

If the tenant goes bankrupt and there is a provision within the tenancy that the tenant will forfeit his right to live in the property if he becomes bankrupt, the landlord can seek a possession order on the basis of the tenant's bankruptcy. It is a matter for the court's discretion whether, contrary to the landlord's wishes, it will allow a bankrupt to remain in his home.

The landlord's bankruptcy is likely to have a greater practical impact. The landlord's interest likewise becomes vested in the trustee-in-bankruptcy, whose duty it is to obtain as much money as he can for the creditors. The trustee will be able to take advantage of any basis on which the landlord might have obtained possession. Often it will be in the creditors' interests to sell the property, if they are able to obtain possession. The resulting proceeds will be much easier to share out than a relatively small periodic rent.

8

LETTING ROOMS AT HOME

From the landlord's perspective

In legal and practical terms the relationship between a home-owner and someone he allows to lodge in his property is very different from that between a landlord who lets a whole house or flat to his tenants. Lodgers are sometimes referred to as paying guests. This description, if slightly archaic, is also apposite.

The lodger is living in someone else's home and it would obviously be very undesirable for any law to give him an entitlement to stay once the home-owner no longer wanted him. The relationship is a personal as much as a financial one and it is right that the law should have very little say in it. In a few rare cases where the lodger moved in before 15 January 1989 and has his own clearly marked territory in the property to which the landlord has very little access, there may be minor restrictions on the landlord obtaining possession. These however amount to a series of procedural hoops for the landlord to go through, which might delay him, rather than a serious barrier to him getting the lodger out. Where such a longstanding relationship has broken down and the tenant is not prepared to move amicably, the landlord should seek legal advice.

Whether to have a lodger

Often the decision to take a lodger is the result of the home-owner's financial need. A spare bedroom is a potential source of income. Many people feel, with considerable justification, that by letting out unused rooms they are performing a socially valuable service. Particularly for young single householders having a lodger can also be attractive as a source of company. Countless life-long friendships and more than a few marriages have grown out of such an arrangement.

For others though, having a lodger would amount to a discomfiting loss of privacy. For people who see it in those terms, unless the financial need is absolutely dire, it is probably best to avoid taking in lodgers. A landlord who resents sharing his home is likely to let that resentment show with the result that there will be two people in close proximity making each other feel uncomfortable.

Generally speaking rents charged to lodgers are a little less than to tenants. To some extent the lodger is receiving a discount for having to live in somebody else's home. This slightly lower rent is largely cancelled out by the tax advantages for people who rent out rooms in their homes.

Before taking a lodger it is advisable to check household insurance policies to ensure that the presence of a lodger is not going to affect their validity.

When considering whether to take someone as a lodger, it is as important to decide whether one could actually get on with that person as it is to consider their reliability in matters such as rent. That is purely a subjective matter and it is worth spending time chatting to the person to establish whether there are common interests and a reasonable personal rapport before making a decision.

Finding a lodger

Finding a lodger should be no harder than finding a tenant. Local newspapers have a role to play, less so perhaps agents. Some institutions are forever searching for rooms. As well as conventional colleges, foreign language schools are a likely source of lodgers particularly in the summer. Maybe friends will know of someone looking for a room. Professional football clubs often want landlords (more usually land-ladies) prepared to take in their apprentices and provide meals and a quasi-parental eye.

Reaching an agreement with the lodger

The rules which the lodger is going to have to respect should be established at the outset. The question of whether overnight guests are going to be allowed should be agreed upon, as should any terms banning the lodger from using certain parts of the property, such as the landlord's bedroom. It is unfair for someone to be allowed to move in and only then be told that there are to be restrictions preventing him using the property as if it were his own home.

Similarly if the landlord is a non-smoker and expects the lodger not to smoke, this should be made clear, and lodgers who would be upset by a smoke-heavy house should make enquiries before committing themselves and finding later that they live in the home of an inconsiderate heavy smoker. Normally the landlord is responsible for paying bills, though the lodger will have to keep a record of and pay for any telephone calls he makes.

It is unwise for either party to commit themselves to an agreement that the lodger should stay for any set period. A month's notice on either side should be sufficient. A formal tenancy agreement is usually not appropriate for a lodger. However a letter of welcome doubling as one setting out "the rules" is a good idea: if things do turn sour, it might help each party know where they stand.

We saw earlier that Mrs Healey had decided to rent out the spare bedroom in Heath Cottage. A rough and ready calculation of the rent for the whole of the cottage came to £154 per week. A lodger sharing the house with just the owner might be expected to pay a little over one-third of that, perhaps £65. To find herself a lodger she placed a card in the window of the nearest shop. As she was not paying by the line she could afford to be rather more effusive than when she was advertising 41a Wilson Road in newspapers.

ROOM TO LET
Room to let in pleasant two bedroom cottage with garden and plenty of living space. Would suit quiet young woman. Non-smoker preferred. Rent £65 per week. Telephone 020 8123 4567

The letter Mrs Healey wrote to Jane whom she took as a lodger read as follows:

Dear Jane,
I am pleased that you have decided to come and live with me at Heath Cottage. The rent as discussed will be £65 per week, which you will pay me every Tuesday in advance. Either of us is entitled to end this arrangement on giving the other four weeks' notice.
You will of course have your own bedroom and be free to

use the rest of the house. I would however ask that you do
not have any guests staying overnight or remaining here
after 11 p.m. unless I have agreed to this in advance. I
would also ask that you and any guests do not smoke any-
where in the house except your own bedroom.
I would ask you to sign a copy of this letter to indicate your
agreement to this.
Best wishes,
Angela Healey

From the tenant's perspective

Being a lodger
From the point of view of the lodger it has to be appreciated that there
is not going to be the same degree of independence as living in a place
that has been let as a separate home by a landlord. The lodger's status is
always at least in part that of a guest, who has to abide by the conven-
tions of his host. If the landlord goes to bed at ten o'clock every night,
the lodger will probably feel a little uneasy staying up and moving
around the house, however quietly, until two o'clock.

If the landlord and lodger don't get on, it will inevitably be the lodger
who has to go. Perhaps because of a lodger's ambiguous status rooms are
usually let at rates around 25% less than would be charged for the equivalent space as a tenant on an equal footing with the other occupants.

A lodger's legal position
The legal position is to an extent a reflection of the lodger's social
position. From the point of view of the law the difference between the
position of a lodger and a tenant is that a lodger has virtually no rights.
If the landlord has agreed in advance to give him a month's notice or if
he is allowed to live there for a specified period, then that agreement
must of course be honoured. If nothing has been said about notice, the
landlord still has to give a reasonable period of notice.

How long this will be will depend largely on how long the lodger has
been there. For one who has been there several years, a month may not
be sufficient. However if only a short time has elapsed, then a shorter

period may be enough. Once that has expired there is no restriction on the landlord's right to possession. Theoretically there need not even be a court order. However evicting a lodger against his will is an extremely risky process. The fact that the landlord was doing so will be no defence against an allegation of assault. Such a course should never be considered without first seeking legal advice.

It is far safer to obtain a court order. There is a procedure which should enable the landlord to obtain a possession order within a matter of weeks if not days. However the landlord is not entitled to start proceedings until any notice period or agreed term of the tenancy has expired.

Flat sharing

Unless a tenancy agreement prohibits sharing, there is no reason why a tenant established in a property cannot take a lodger rather than share the tenancy with the lodger. Sharing the tenancy requires the approval of the landlord and may mean that the newcomer has as many rights as the original tenant. If someone has been living in a place a long time he may be unwilling to do this. Sometimes however the prospective newcomer may express a reluctance to agree to be a lodger rather than a joint tenant. A possible compromise might be to agree that the lodger should become a tenant after a trial period, if he and the original tenant are still getting along.

If a lodger is required to pay more than half the amount of rent the tenant is paying to the landlord, he may well feel resentful. Whilst a tenant who takes such a high rent from a lodger could be accused of being greedy, little can be done to prevent him from doing so.

Whilst the lodger's legal position may be vastly different from a tenant's the human issues of people having to live in close proximity are much the same whether one is another's lodger or they are sharing on a legally equal basis.

Sharing a property often works better when it is done by a group of strangers who have joined up for the purpose of sharing rather than a group of friends who move in together. Often people assume their friends will have the same outlook on matters as they do. However just because people find each other very good company in the pub and at college does not mean they will have the same views on how soon after eating washing up should be done.

The doing of chores like the washing up, wandering around the house undressed, walking into other people's rooms without knocking, the division of bills, the playing of loud music, using the bathroom for long periods in the morning, bolting doors at night and the unauthorised borrowing of property are just a few of the things over which people can fall out. When strangers move in together everybody tends to be on their best behaviour until all occupants have got to know each other properly, by which time an unspoken consensus about what is and isn't acceptable has been arrived at.

Whether the house is shared with complete strangers or with people one has known since primary school, it is always better to deal with any resentments by bringing them up in good humoured way as soon as they arise rather than let them build up until an explosive abusive row at some later stage.

9

ENDING THE TENANCY

From the landlord's perspective

It is easier to gain a practical understanding of the rules that apply to possession orders if one has a grasp of the very basic legal principles underlying them. For a landlord to obtain possession he needs to show two things:

> *a) that the tenant no longer has a contractual right to be in possession of the premises*
> *b) that one of the statutory grounds or basis for granting possession has arisen*

Where a tenancy is granted for a fixed term, the contractual right ends when that term expires. However so long as the tenant remains in possession of the property he does so as a statutory periodic tenant. No statutory periodic tenancy will arise where
· the tenancy has ended because of a court order
· the tenant has, himself, terminated the tenancy
· the landlord and tenant enter into a new agreement which involves the tenant being given possession of the same, or substantially the same, premises

A statutory periodic tenancy continues automatically until it is ended. It will contain standard implied terms which are automatically fixed according to the terms of the preceding tenancy (that is, all the terms and conditions of the tenancy agreement before the term expired). It may be ended upon any of the grounds for possession applicable to assured tenancies granted after 14 January 1989. A statutory periodic tenancy cannot be assigned.

If there is a forfeiture clause and the tenant does something that entitles the landlord to forfeit the lease, that will end the tenant's contractual right even if the term of the tenancy has not expired (although if the tenancy is an assured shorthold granted after 28 February 1997 the landlord will have to wait for a minimum of six months to have elapsed since the start of the tenancy).

When this situation arises and the landlord needs to rely on a forfeiture clause for breach of a term other than for the payment of rent, he must first serve a notice on the tenant requiring him to remedy the breach. The procedure relating to such a notice is complex and drafting one is a skilled job. An account of how to do that is outside the scope of this book, and any landlord finding he needs to serve such a notice would be well advised to consult a solicitor.

Where a tenancy is not for a specific period but merely has been renewed automatically every week or every month the landlord need not do anything more than serve the notice appropriate to the type of tenancy to end the tenant's contractual right. Different forms of notice have to be served depending upon whether the tenancy was granted before (a protected tenancy) or after (an assured tenancy) 15 January 1989.

If the tenant is still living at the premises, the landlord will have to show that one of these statutory basis for ordering possession applies. These are different depending on whether the tenancy was granted before or after 14 January 1989. If the tenant ceases to live in the property, it will be sufficient for the landlord to merely show he has the contractual right. The tenant's statutory protection will no longer apply and it will not be necessary for the landlord to show a statutory basis.

Often tenants are happy for the landlord to have possession but some want him first to obtain a court order. If he has obtained such a court order, the tenant is then more likely to be entitled to local authority housing. If he left voluntarily, he would be "intentionally homeless" which would make it far harder for him to be rehoused by a local authority. Landlords may resent being put through the process of obtaining a possession order from the court for this reason although there is little they can do about it.

As a general rule courts are inclined not to make outright orders for possession when there is merely a discretion to do so. County court judges are acutely aware of the problems caused by homelessness and whilst not necessarily unsympathetic to the position of a landlord who has an unwanted tenant, consider his suffering the lesser of two evils. If there are arrears of rent, a compromise is often reached by making a suspended possession order. This effectively means a landlord will become entitled to possession only if the tenant fails to pay the rent in future. Similarly, if possession is applied for on the basis of some other form of misbehaviour on the part of the tenant, the court may suspend the order on the condition that the tenant does not repeat the misconduct. There is no power to suspend the possession order when a mandatory ground for possession applies.

Grounds for possession under assured tenancies granted after 14 January 1989

The basis on which a court can order possession in respect of tenancies granted after 14 January 1989 are listed in Schedule 2 of the Housing Act 1988. They are known as Grounds and are divided into two categories: mandatory and discretionary.

Grounds 1 to 8 are mandatory, which means if they exist and the landlord has complied with the correct procedures, the court has to make a possession order. Grounds 9 to 17 are discretionary, giving the court a choice whether or not it is reasonable to grant possession when they apply. Unless the landlord relies upon Ground 8 (arrears of rent being due both when proceedings were served and at the date of the hearing) the court can give permission for the landlord to add or alter any of the grounds upon which he seeks to rely.

1. Non payment of rent

There are three different statutory grounds for possession based on non-payment of rent. These are:

a) that the rent is in arrears at the time the notice that the landlord intends seeking possession was served *and* at the time of the court hearing (Ground 8)

b) that there are some arrears of rent both when the notice was served and at the time proceedings were commenced (Ground 10)

c) that the tenant has persistently delayed in paying rent (Ground 11)

Ground 8 relates to a more extreme state of affairs than the other two and when it applies, the others almost certainly will too. If Ground 8 does apply, the court must order possession, whereas the others merely give the court a discretion to do so.

Ground 8 cannot be enforced unless a minimum amount of rent arrears has accrued, the amount dependent upon the frequency rent should have been paid. The table below sets out the minimum amount of unpaid rent that is needed before a landlord may utilise Ground 8.

Frequency	Minimum arrears
Weekly	*8 weeks' unpaid*
Fortnightly	*8 weeks' unpaid*
Monthly	*2 months' unpaid*
Quarterly	*One quarter's rent unpaid, more than 3 months overdue*
Annually	*3 months' rent unpaid, more than 3 months overdue.*

If an action is begun on the basis of Ground 8, there is always a possibility that the tenant will pay off the arrears, or at least reduce them enough to fall below the minimum. If that does happen, the court will consider making a possession order on the basis of the other Grounds.

Ground 10 differs from Ground 8 (aside from it being discretionary) as there is no particular amount of rent that needs to be in arrears. All that is necessary is for there to be rent in arrears at the date proceedings were brought. Thus a tenant is not able to avoid this ground (though he may be able to avoid Ground 8) by paying the amounts due before the hearing. This highlights the importance of not relying solely upon one ground where others may also be utilised.

2. Other misbehaviour by the tenant

There are four grounds, all of which are discretionary, which deal with misconduct on the part of the tenant other than that relating to the non-payment of rent. The Housing Act 1996 extended the scope. The four grounds are:

1) the tenant has broken one or more of the conditions of the tenancy, other than one related to the payment of rent (Ground 12)

2) the property has deteriorated because of the actions of the tenant or anyone living with him (unless the tenant is taking proper steps to get rid of that person) (Ground 13)

3) the tenant or anyone living with him or visiting the property has

(a) been guilty of conduct that has constituted a nuisance to a person living, visiting or otherwise engaging in a lawful activity in the locality the occupiers of adjoining property or

(b) i) been convicted of using the property or allowing it to be used for immoral or illegal purposes or

(ii) been convicted of an arrestable offence committed either in or in the locality of the property (Ground 14)

4) the condition of the furniture (provided by the landlord) has deteriorated because of the actions of the tenant or anyone living with him (unless the tenant is taking proper steps to get rid of that person) (Ground 15)

A tenant who keeps pets in the property when the lease contains a prohibition on doing so is likely to find he is the subject of an application pursuant to Ground 12, for instance. If the lease contains terms prohibiting the tenant from causing damage or nuisance, this Ground will apply equally with 13 or 14 if the tenant indulges in such behaviour. In practical terms the landlord is in no better a position whether an action of the tenant offends one or more Grounds. On the other hand if by separate actions, the tenant has managed to breach more than one Ground or the same Ground more than once, the court is less likely to exercise its discretion not to make a possession order.

The most frequent and obvious form of nuisance by the tenant is making too much noise. If there are complaints from neighbours that the tenant has been persistently disturbing them, then the court may well be prepared to make a possession order notwithstanding the normal reluctance to render someone homeless. On the other hand, a landlord who brings an action based on one loud party is highly unlikely to succeed.

Where there is damage to the property, the court will also have regard to the degree of damage and to the tenant's willingness to make good.

3. <u>Where a false statement has been made by the tenant or a person acting on his behalf</u>

This new discretionary ground was added by the Housing Act 1996. The ground provides that the landlord may recover possession if he was was induced to grant the tenancy by a false statement made knowingly or recklessly by a tenant or a person acting at the tenant's instigation (Ground 17).

It does not matter whether the tenancy was granted to a number of people and only one person made the false statement. It will be necessary, however, for the landlord to show that he would not have granted the tenancy had he known the true state of affairs.

4. <u>Where the landlord has served a notice before the tenancy began</u>

The situations where a landlord is entitled to serve a notice which will in some situations give him an automatic right to possession when the tenancy expires have already been discussed. Leaving aside assured shorthold tenancies which will be dealt with separately, much the most important of these is Ground 1 where the landlord has lived in the premises himself or intends to do so in future. If the landlord actually has lived in the premises, then there is nothing more for him to prove to obtain possession on this ground. If he has not lived there before, he will have to show that he (or his spouse) now requires the property as his only or principal home.

There are no restrictions in place as to the reasons for which a landlord may want to serve a notice of his intention to recover possession under this ground. A new landlord who purchased the property during the currency of the tenancy is unable to rely upon this ground. With Ground 1, like all the others discussed under this heading, the making of a possession order is mandatory.

If the landlord was entitled to serve a Ground 1 notice but failed to do so, then the court may if it is just and equitable dispense with the notice. This is most likely to be done where the landlord had told the tenant that it had been his own home or might be in future but had forgotten to actually serve a formal notice. In that situation it would be harsh to deprive the landlord of his home.

On the other hand if the landlord had said nothing to the tenant about such matters it would be unfair for the tenant to be evicted. The court has the same discretion where a landlord has lost his interest to his mortgagee, which is claiming possession under Ground 2. However in that situation it is much less likely to exercise the discretion against the tenant.

In the rare cases where a landlord has been entitled to serve a notice under one of the Grounds 3 to 5 there is no discretion at all to dispense with the notice.

5. Redevelopment

If the landlord wishes to demolish or reconstruct or carry out substantial works on the property, this will in some circumstances entitle him to possession (Ground 6). This is by far the most complicated of the statutory grounds. Landlords considering such work should consult a solicitor to find out if this condition may apply to them as should tenants faced with a claim by a landlord for possession on this basis. Possession will only be granted if it is not practical for the tenant to remain in occupation of some or all of the property while the works are being carried on, or if he is not willing to continue living there on that basis.

If possession is ordered on this ground, the landlord will have to pay the tenant's reasonable removal expenses. There is no requirement for the landlord to serve a notice about his intention to redevelop before the tenancy starts. Like Ground 1, a new landlord who purchased the property during the currency of the tenancy is unable to avail himself of this ground.

6. Suitable Alternative Accommodation

If there is somewhere else available for the tenant to live, this may be a reason for making a possession order under Ground 9. Usually the alternative accommodation will be somewhere offered by the present landlord but it does not need to be. Accommodation provided by the local authority or even owned by the tenant himself could be sufficient.

In considering this ground the court first has to decide if the alternative accommodation actually is suitable. Relevant to this is are matters such as the size of the property, the rent, how convenient it is for the tenant's work and the sort of furniture that will be provided.

If the court does consider it suitable, it will usually exercise its discretion to make an order in favour of the landlord. However in some cases it might feel so sorry for the tenant as to take the opposite course. An elderly person who was distressed at having to move from a long-standing home would be the obvious example.

A person who has become strongly immersed in the social life of an area or a block of flats might be able to persuade a court not to make a possession order forcing him to live somewhere else. Considerations like these would of course have to be balanced against any hardship caused to the landlord by declining to grant the possession order.

As with the redevelopment ground, if a court makes a possession order on this basis it will order the landlord to pay the tenant's reasonable removal expenses.

7. Termination of Employment

Where the property was let as a consequence of the tenant's employment and that employment ends possession may be ordered pursuant to Ground 16. If the tenant was allowed to live in the property because doing so was essential for him to perform his duties, there would not have been a tenancy at all and the landlord's task will be that much simpler.

However, if the landlord owns property near, say, a factory that he lets out to his employees in the hope of making it easier for them to get to work on time there will be a tenancy. In that instance this Ground 16 is likely to apply. The mere fact that the tenant has made an application to an employment tribunal and seeks to be reinstated to his job will not adjourn the landlord's claim under this ground.

In exercising its discretion the court is likely to take into account the reason the employee left. One who was dismissed without a good reason will generally be treated more sympathetically than one who has resigned or been sacked for misconduct.

8. Death of the tenant

Where the tenancy was granted after 14 January 1989 and the tenant dies, the tenancy comes to an end. However the tenancy may pass under his will or his intestacy. If the person to whom it passes is not living in the premises the landlord is automatically entitled to possession because it would not then be a residential tenancy. In practice, tenants rarely think of tenancies as assets which can be left in wills.

If a tenant makes a will which makes no specific reference to the tenancy it will pass to the person who has been left the residue of the estate. Intestacy is the most likely means by which the tenancy may pass. If the person to whom the tenancy passes is living in the premises he will become the tenant.

In some circumstances the person who becomes a tenant will have the right to succeed to the tenancy. If those circumstances do not apply, the landlord will have an automatic right to possession under the mandatory Ground 7. To be able to rely on this the landlord must commence proceedings within a year of the tenant's death or, if later, (subject to the court's discretion) within a year of finding out about that death. The landlord may accept rent during that time without losing his rights under Ground 7. However if he agrees in writing to a change in the terms of the tenancy, perhaps increasing the rent, during that period a new assured tenancy, to which Ground 7 will not apply, will be created.

Giving notice to end tenancies granted after 14 January 1989

Before the landlord can obtain possession of a property he has to serve a notice on the tenant warning him of his intention to seek possession. There is nothing to prevent him merely asking the tenant informally to go either by letter or even just speaking to him. However, if the tenant stays, the landlord will have to obtain a court order and it will be necessary to have served the notice to do this.

Such notice has to be on the official form. If there is more than one tenant, it must be addressed to both or all of them.

Only under Ground 14 is there no minimum notice period necessary. One can start proceedings with Ground 14 once notice has been served. For all the other grounds, a minimum amount of notice needs to pass before proceedings can be brought. For some Grounds a landlord needs to give at least two months' notice. These are where:

a) the landlord has previously lived or intends living in the premises (Ground 1)

b) a mortgagee seeks possession on the basis of a Ground 1 notice (Ground 2)

c) the property is required for a minister of religion, the appropriate notice having been given before the tenancy commenced (Ground 5)

d) a new tenancy was created on the death of the previous tenant (Ground 6)

e) the landlord wants to redevelop the property (Ground 7)

f) the landlord is relying on suitable alternative accommodation being available (Ground 9)

g) where the property was let in consequence of the tenant's employment (Ground 16)

In other cases the landlord needs only give two weeks' notice (Grounds 3,4,8,10,11,12,13,15 and 17). However if the tenancy is one where the tenant pays rent every month, the landlord will have to give a month's notice starting from the date when rent is next due. If rent is paid quarterly, he will have to give a quarter's notice no matter what grounds are relied upon.

The landlord may rely upon more than one ground, but will have to give the longer period of notice if any of the grounds which require it are specified. Thus if a landlord is seeking possession against a tenant because of a continual nuisance, he may use Ground 12 and Ground 14; although there is no notice period required for Ground 14, the landlord is also using Ground 12 so he must give at least two weeks' notice - the longer period of notice. The landlord must always specify which grounds he is relying upon and set out what each ground is.

Once the notice is served, the landlord has twelve months to commence proceedings. The court is more likely to exercise its discretion in favour of the landlord if he has begun proceedings shortly after serving the notice, particularly if a claim is based on grounds relating to the tenant's misconduct.

If the landlord fails to serve the notice, the court may still make a possession order. Once again the court has to consider whether it is just and equitable to dispense with the notice. If the landlord has told the tenant that he was seeking possession, but not served any notice it is more likely that the court would be willing to dispense with the notice.

If the tenant has had no warning at all of the landlord's intention, then it is highly unlikely that the notice would be dispensed with. If on the other hand the notice was served but contained a minor defect, it would probably be treated as valid under this provision.

There is no power to dispense with the notice in a claim based on Ground 8 (two months' arrears of rent). However even if that ground cannot be relied upon in the absence of a proper notice, the court could usually still make a possession order on the other rent grounds (10 and 11).

Possession under assured shorthold tenancies

The landlord has an automatic right to possession at the end of the term of an assured shorthold tenancy and does not need to show that any of the statutory grounds apply. The landlord must give at least two month's notice in writing to the tenant, or if appropriate both or all of the tenants, that he requires possession. The notice may be given before the fixed term has finished but must not expire until after then.

For example, if the tenancy expires on 31 July 2001, the landlord could serve notice on 31 May 2001 to expire on the same date as the tenancy. Notice can be given at any time after the expiry of the fixed term, provided at least 6 months have elapsed since the start of the tenancy, if the tenant carries on living at the premises, but notice still needs to give the tenant at least two months' warning. Notice which expires after the term of the tenancy has ended must expire on a date when the tenant is due to pay rent. The notice need not be in any particular form.

The accelerated possession procedure

This is, as its name suggests, a faster way for a landlord to gain possession of the property. It provides the landlord with a (fairly) straightforward method that may enable him to avoid the delays and further expenses of a court hearing. It can be used where the tenancy is

(a) an assured shorthold - the landlord claims under section 21 of the Housing Act 1998. There is no need for any grounds to be specified

(b) an assured tenancy - the landlord claims under section 8 of the Housing Act. The landlord must rely upon one of the mandatory grounds (Grounds 1, 3, 4, 5). The landlord must also have previously given the tenant a notice that he might claim possession under one of the grounds four months before the tenancy ends and also a notice under section 8 of the Housing Act 1996, sent at least two months before the tenancy expires, which states that he intended to apply to the court for possession.

Two conditions need to be satisfied before the procedure can be used. First, there must be a written tenancy agreement. Secondly, the tenant must have been given the required notice in writing that the landlord seeks possession. Unless the court considers a hearing necessary, it will make its decision, without a hearing, based on the evidence that is provided by each party. It is essential, therefore, that all written evidence that is needed and relied upon is provided at the outset.

The procedure can only be used to gain possession and the landlord can only recover the costs of making the application. If there are rent arrears a landlord cannot use the accelerated method to effect possession.

However, if the term of the tenancy has expired it is possible for the landlord to utilise the accelerated possession procedure and then, if desired, take a separate claim for any monies owed.

Grounds for possession under tenancies granted before 15 January 1989

Where the tenancy was granted before 15 January 1989, there are Cases instead of grounds for possession. These are listed in Schedule 15 to the Rent Act 1977 and two other basis that are listed in other parts of that Act. Although there are twenty-one situations where possession can be granted, these apply in a considerably narrower range of circumstance than did the seventeen under the Housing Act 1988. Cases 1 to 10 are discretionary (Case 7 has been repealed), Cases 11 to 20 are mandatory. The court has similar powers to suspend possession orders as it does for later tenancies.

1. <u>Non-payment of rent</u>

Where there are any rent arrears the court has a discretion to make an order for possession (Case 1). This Case also covers any other breaches of the tenancy agreement by the tenant, such as keeping a pet when one is prohibited.

2. <u>Other misbehaviour by the tenant</u>

Cases 2, 3 and 4 cover very similar situations to those described under the same heading in respect of tenancies subject to the Housing Act 1988 and Grounds 13, 14 and 15 respectively. There are other Cases which loosely fit under this heading. These are:

a) the tenant has given notice to quit and then changes his mind but the landlord has already taken steps to relet or sell the property (Case 5)

b) the tenant sublets the whole of the property without the landlord's consent (Case 6)

c) the tenant sublets part of the property at a higher rent than he is paying himself in respect of that part (Case 10)

3. <u>Where the landlord has served a notice before the tenancy commenced</u>

The most frequent situation in which the landlord can serve a notice is when he has lived in the property previously and subsequently required it as a residence for himself or a member of his family (Case 11). A mortgagee who has taken over the landlord's interest can claim possession under this Case, as can the person to whom the property passed on the landlord's death. A landlord who wants to sell the property so that he can use the proceeds to buy a home nearer to where he works can also rely on it.

If a landlord bought a home he intended to live in after retiring from work, he could serve a notice under Case 12. On retirement he would then be able to recover possession in similar circumstances to those which applied under Case 11. Case 12 though did not extend to the situation where he required for the property as a residence for his family members rather than himself.

Case 20 provides for members of the regular armed forces to be able to let property without necessarily having lived there first and recover them in similar circumstances to Case 11. This Case also did not extend to situations where recovery was sought because the landlord wanted to provide a residence for members of his family rather than himself.

Cases 13 to 18 enabled notices to be served in less common situations such as out of season holiday lettings and lettings of property usually used by ministers of religion.

Case 19 applies where there was a protected shorthold tenancy. In many ways this was similar to a shorthold assured tenancy. Advance notice had to be served on the tenant, informing him the property was to be let as an assured shorthold. It had to be a term for between one and five years. If the tenant continued in occupation after the expiry of the term the landlord retains his rights to obtain possession.

In respect of Cases 11, 12, 19 and 20, if notice was not served before the commencement of the tenancy the landlord might be able persuade the court to order possession nonetheless. The court's discretion to do this would be exercised on the same principles as it would be in considering an application under Housing Act 1988 Ground 1 discussed earlier. Significantly there was a discretion to dispense with the initial notice requirement in relation to a protected shorthold tenancy although there is no such power in relation to an assured shorthold tenancy.

4. Termination of employment

Case 8, provides the landlord with a potential right to possession in similar circumstances to Ground 16 discussed under the same heading in relation to the Housing Act 1988. However for Case 8 to apply the landlord must also now require the property to be let to another employee in addition to the fact that it was let to the present tenant in consequence of his employment.

5. Landlord's requirements for the property

If the landlord wants the property as a home for himself his parents or his children then that may be sufficient to justify a possession order (Case 9). This Case will not normally be available to a landlord who bought his interest in the property after the tenancy was granted by the previous owner.

6. Suitable Alternative Accommodation

Section 98 of the Rent Act 1977 contains a discretionary ground for ordering possession that applies in very similar circumstances to those applicable when the landlord makes such a claim under the Housing Act 1988. The requirement to pay the tenant's removal costs does not, however, apply.

7. Overcrowding

Where the property becomes overcrowded within the statutory definition the landlord has a mandatory right to possession (s101 Rent Act 1977). This definition is exceedingly complex and outside the scope of this book. It is likely to apply if people of the opposite sex over the age of ten, other than couples, have to share a room.

Giving notice to end tenancies granted before 15 January 1989

In some circumstances a notice to quit is required to terminate a tenancy granted before 15 January 1989. If the tenancy has never been for a fixed term, then the notice will be necessary. This will be the case where it was originally agreed that the tenant would be rent on a weekly or monthly basis indefinitely and he has carried on doing so.

If the tenancy has been for a fixed term, say one year, and has expired with the tenant remaining in occupation, the notice will not be necessary but it may be advisable to serve one anyway. A notice to quit must contain specified information. It must, if rent is paid weekly, give at least

28 days' notice effective from the date the next instalment is due. If rent is paid monthly or quarterly, then those periods are the minimum periods of notice. Yearly tenancies however require only six months' notice. If there is more than one tenant it must be addressed to all or both of them.

To give an example, suppose a tenant pays rent every Monday. On Wednesday 3rd July 2000 the landlord decides to serve a notice to quit. He can serve the notice immediately but it must give 28 days' notice from Monday 8th July, the date when the next rent is due. That notice should therefore expire on Monday 5th August. If the tenant paid rent monthly on the first of the month, then notice given on 3rd July should expire on 1 September, one month after the date the next paymen is due.

If a notice to quit is not served when needed, the court has no discretion to order possession. As the landlord had no right to possession when he started the action, his claim cannot succeed and will be thrown out.

Evicting the tenant without a court order

However tempting it may be; however much a landlord may feel he has been abused by a tenant; however frustrated he is by delays in the legal system, a landlord should not even think about evicting a tenant without a court order. If he does, he will incur the ire of the civil and often the criminal law. The type of tenant who has reduced the landlord to this level of anger will inevitably relish being able to use the legal system to exact revenge upon the landlord.

The Protection from Eviction Act 1977 makes virtually any form of harassment of a tenant by a landlord or his agent serious offences. This can apply to acts far short of actually evicting the tenant. The law makes it an offence to do any of the following things intending, knowing or having cause to believe that these would cause a tenant to leave his home or part of it or not do anything he could normally expect to do. It is an offence for the landlord (or anyone acting on his behalf) to:

· *do acts likely to interfere with the tenant's quiet enjoyment (violence, threats of violence and persistent oral abuse are some examples of harassment)*

· *do acts likely to interfere with the peace or comfort of anyone living with the tenant*

· *persistently withdraw or withhold services which the tenant has a reasonable need to live in the premises as a home (electricity or water is sufficient)*

If the landlord does find himself being prosecuted for such behaviour, the matter can be tried either by magistrates or by a jury: usually the accused landlord will at least get the dubious honour of choosing which. On conviction by magistrates, the landlord may get six months' imprisonment and/or a fine of up to £2,500. In the Crown Court that can be two years and/or an unlimited fine. Of course, only in extreme cases are maximum penalties or any form of imprisonment imposed.

An illegally evicted tenant will also have a civil claim for damages. He will be entitled to compensation for any financial loss suffered. If, for instance, after being evicted he had to stay in a hotel until he could find another place to rent, the landlord will be ordered to reimburse his bills. If his possessions are damaged or lost in the course of the eviction the landlord will have to replace them. On top of this there will be damages to compensate him for the sheer unpleasantness of losing his home. If he has been assaulted or threatened in the process of the eviction, these damages will rocket.

Finally, in an effort to ensure the landlord does not gain from his illegal action the law will require the landlord to pay to the tenant the difference between the market value of the premises when they were subject to the tenancy and when they were not. Where there is a tenant who had the benefit of the protection of the Rent Act 1977 because the tenancy was granted before 15 January 1989, this can amount to getting on for half the value of the premises. If the tenant gets back into possession whether or not as a result of a court order, the landlord will not have to pay this head of damages.

Even once the landlord has obtained a possession order, an attempt to evict a tenant except pursuant to a warrant, which is issued separately by the court and executed by certified bailiffs is still illegal for these purposes.

The law is less draconian if the landlord and the tenant share accommodation at the premises and the premises constitute the landlord's only or main home. However even in those circumstances evicting someone without a court order would be asking for trouble. Regardless of the niceties of landlord and tenant law, the landlord would lay himself open to allegations of assault and stealing the tenant's possessions. If either a landlord or a tenant believes that a wrongful eviction claim may have arisen he would be well advised to see a solicitor.

From the tenant's perspective

Actions by mortgagees

If the landlord served a Ground 1 notice in respect of a tenancy granted after 14 January 1989 a mortgagee who takes possession of the property will also be able to rely on the notice. A mortgagee is most likely to be able to do this where a landlord has fallen into arrears with his payments. Even if the landlord has failed to serve the notice but could have served it, the court may order possession in these circumstances. In practice, it is less likely to do so than where the landlord himself is seeking possession having forgotten to serve the notice. If the landlord granted the tenancy without seeking the consent of his mortgagee and did so in breach of his mortgage agreement, the tenant may not even be entitled to remain in possession until the end of the contractual term.

Mortgagees who have taken possession of premises are sometimes willing for tenants to remain in occupation so long of course as the tenants are willing to continue paying rent to the mortgagees. Evicting tenants who have behaved entirely properly has sometimes brought bad publicity upon banks and building societies. To avoid this, such organisations are often willing to allow a reasonably long period for the tenant to remain in the property. Used subtly the threat of publicity may be fairly productive. Banks and building societies often possess incredibly inefficient legal departments and may, even if not prepared to negotiate with the tenants, take months to commence possession proceedings.

When the landlord sells his interest in the property the purchaser will not be able to rely on the Ground 1 notice.

The fact that a mortgagee requires possession was one of the circumstances in which possession could be obtained under a tenancy granted before 15 January 1989. This was dependent upon there having been a Case 11 notice or the court believing it would be fair to dispense with such a notice.

When the tenant wishes to terminate the agreement

A tenancy for a fixed term obliges the tenant to pay rent throughout the period of the term. Just as the landlord is not be entitled to evict a tenant until the term has run out, the tenant is not able to leave. In practice it may well be that most landlords would not bother taking any action if a tenant did walk out, but that of course does not alter the tenant's legal and moral obligations.

Many tenancy agreements have the effect of preventing the tenant getting out of his obligations even by finding a replacement. However, in practice, if the tenant finds a reasonably respectable person willing to take his place, it would be ridiculous for the landlord to refuse it. Should the landlord attempt to recover the rent for the remainder of the period from the tenant, his claim may well be disallowed because he has then failed to mitigate his loss. In this situation it is the tenant rather than the landlord who should go to the trouble and expense of finding the replacement tenant. Should another tenant be found but subsequently fail to pay rent, the landlord will still be entitled to look to the original tenant for reimbursement during the remainder of the term.

In the case of a tenancy that is not for a fixed period the tenant must give at least four weeks' notice to bring it to an end. This notice must expire on a day when rent is otherwise due to paid. The notice given by the tenant must be in writing but need not follow any particular form. A simple letter is the best way to do it.

An example of such a letter sent in February 2001 might be:

Dear Landlord,

I am writing to let you know I shall be leaving the property on 31 March 2001. Perhaps you could please contact me to discuss the necessary arrangements and to return my deposit.

Yours sincerely,

10

GOING TO COURT

The Civil Procedure Rules

The Civil Procedure Rules 1998 ("CPR") apply to all proceedings commenced on or after 26 April 1999. These rules made significant changes to the procedures dealing with civil claims. Previously, parties involved in civil disputes often kept their "cards close to their chests". The CPR altered the way in which litigation should be pursued so that nowadays parties are encouraged to "put their cards on the table". There are also clearer procedures so as to encourage settlement. The CPR's overriding objective is to ensure that cases are dealt with justly and, with this in mind it seeks to ensure that all parties are on equal footing.

CPR 1.1 provides:

These rules are a new procedural code with the overriding objective of enabling the court to deal with cases justly.

(Dealing with cases justly includes, so far as is practicable – ensuring that the parties are on an equal footing; saving expense; dealing with the case in ways which are proportionate:

    (i) to the amount of money involved;

    (ii) to the importance of the case;

    (iii) to the complexity of issues; and

    (iv) to the financial position of each party

ensuring that it is dealt with expeditiously and fairly; and allotting to it an appropriate share of the court's resources, whilst taking into account the need to allot resources to other cases.)

In general the CPR has not affected the procedures (and, save for certain changes in terminology and layout, the forms) used by landlords and tenants in going to court.

From the landlord's perspective

The county court

Claims for possession of residential premises should almost invariably be brought in the county court. The procedure for starting a possession action varies depending on the basis on which possession is claimed. There are four different procedures, each of which will be discussed separately. Whichever procedure is used the landlord should first decide in which county court he is going to start the case . There are around 300 different such courts in England & Wales, each having a specific geographical area. They are listed in the phone books.

Proceedings should be begun in the court which covers the area in which the property is situated. It is not always easy to find out which court covers which area (this particularly so in London). If an action is begun in the wrong court, that court will either accept jurisdiction or transfer the proceedings to the correct court. But the latter task can take several weeks. A telephone enquiry beforehand should establish whether the court you have in mind is the correct court for that location.

It will often be necessary to visit the county court to obtain the correct form to enable proceedings to be started. If the form can be completed there and then, asking a member of the court staff to check it may decrease the likelihood of it being rejected because it has been incorrectly completed.

The person bringing the claim is the Claimant and it is brought against the Defendant.

 A fee has to be paid on commencement of proceedings. If the claim is for possession alone, that fee is at the time of writing £120. If arrears of rent or damages are claimed (perhaps for damage caused to the property) then the fee will be:

Up£200 - £27	Up to £300 - £38
Up to £400 - £50	Up to £500 - £60
Up to £1,000 - £80	Up to £5,000 - £115
Up to £15,000 - £230	Up to £50,000 - £350
Over £50,000 - £350	

(The value of the claims above exclude interest)

If a landlord wishes to serve a claim form personally, he should express this intention when paying the court fee. The Court will then return (or post back) the form for the landlord to serve personally.

Rent arrears cases

The forms by which landlords start actions for possession orders where there are arrears of rent have been simplified. This appears to have been done with the aim of reducing legal costs and making it easier for landlords who wish to proceed without a solicitor at all.

There is now a printed county court form on which the landlord submits details of his case. The form is titled "Particulars of claim for possession (rented property)" (It is also called form N119). The form can also be used where the landlord seeks to rely on other grounds that do not relate to rent. Instructions on filling in the form are provided in the form's left-hand margin.

Possession pursuant to notice served before the tenancy was granted

Where, if the tenancy was granted before 28 February 1997, the landlord has served a notice before the tenancy was granted saying it was an assured shorthold tenancy or that Ground 1 applied then the procedure for obtaining possession can be much simpler and shorter without the need for any hearing at all.

A mortgagee claiming possession under Ground 2 cannot use this procedure. The landlord starts the action on a standard form available from the county court (form N5). This form once completed is an affidavit, which means the landlord has to swear it. Swearing an affidavit can be done in the court office or in front of a solicitors. Solicitors will charge a nominal fee for this.

The form contains well drafted explanatory notes which specify which of the many alternatives it provides should be deleted in any particular situation. Filling it in should not present any problems but as with any form that asks a lot of questions and involves a degree of cross-referencing it is easy to become confused. The importance of setting aside time to do the form properly cannot be stressed enough. It will be necessary to provide copies of the notices and exhibit them to the affidavit. This means the person in front of whom the affidavit is sworn verifies the fact that these copies are attached.

Once the form is submitted and sent on by the court to the tenant he has fourteen days to reply. If no reply is received, the landlord can then request the court to make a possession order. If the tenant does reply, raising a matter which leads the judge considering the papers to believe he could have a defence to the claim, a hearing will be ordered. If the tenant's reply does not raise anything of substance, a possession order will be made without any hearing.

Landlords cannot use this procedure if they are also claiming rent arrears. If there are arrears of rent, they can still use this procedure to obtain possession then start a fresh action for rent arrears. Alternatively they can start an action under the general procedure claiming both possession and arrears of rent. In practice a landlord will rarely actually obtain rent arrears from a tenant after he has been evicted.

There is a similar procedure for pre-15 January 1989 tenancies (see elsewhere in this book) where notices which entitle the landlord to possession were served before the tenancy commenced. If this procedure is used, the hearing can be at any time after fourteen days of the court having received the form - in some cases seven days. The application has to be made on a specified form. The type of form depends on the basis on which the notice was served. It must be accompanied by an affidavit which sets out the basis on which the landlord is claiming possession and it must exhibit the relevant documents.

As with the procedure for later tenancies, rent cannot be recovered, though it can be the subject of a separate action.

Squatters

Where the occupants of the property are not and have never been tenants, the owner may use a procedure that is designed to enable him to obtain a possession order very quickly. This procedure is designed primarily to remove squatters. It would not be appropriate in a case where someone has been granted a "licence" because the property owner hoped to avoid giving statutory protection to the tenants. As a device for getting rid of lodgers it will often succeed, but if the lodger has been in the property for a long time, the court may insist on the landlord using the general procedure discussed in the next section.

In cases of tremendous urgency it is sometimes better to commence the action using this procedure in the High Court where a hearing date may be available more quickly. A property owner contemplating such a course will, however, need the help of a solicitor. The application is commenced on the form N312. This form is sent to the court along with an affidavit which must state the following:

> *a) whether the Claimant owns the land as freeholder, leaseholder or has some other interest*
>
> *b) the circumstances in which it is being occupied without his permission*
>
> *c) that he does not know the name of any person occupying the land other than those he has named as the Defendants*
>
> *d) a statement of truth at the end*

In the case of squatters, whose names the landlord does not know, the Defendants can be referred to as "persons unknown". This application has to be served in a way that will draw it to the occupier's attention. Usually the court will arrange that. If it cannot do so or is likely to cause a long delay, it will be necessary for the property owner to instruct a solicitor.

A hearing should be arranged by the court within a week or so of the papers being sent to the tenants. At this hearing the judge will read the Claimant's papers and give the Defendant a chance to say what he wants by way of reply. If it transpires that there are arguments as to why the occupier might be entitled to remain in possession, a full hearing will be ordered. If there clearly is no defence the court will order possession usually with immediate effect. Such an order will not however be enforced immediately.

Other cases, the general procedure

Where possession is not claimed on the basis of rent arrears or a notice of the sort discussed above, the action is started by the landlord using the general county court form (N4) applicable to what are known as fixed date actions. As well as straightforward details, this needs to contain a statement of why the landlord believes he is entitled to possession known as the Particulars of Claim. Drafting this is quite a skilled job and many landlords do seek the help of a solicitor to do it. The particulars must give the following information:

> *a) the fact that the Claimant is the landlord and the Defendant the tenant*

b) when the tenancy commenced

c) which of the statutory Grounds or Cases for possession apply (if the landlord claims there is not in fact a tenancy he should say so)

d) the details those Grounds or Cases applicable

e) the date when any notice seeking possession or notice to quit was served and when it took effect

f) details of any damages the landlord is claiming

g) the fact that the landlord seeks possession and (if appropriate) damages

h) if a large amount of money is owing, the landlord should also request interest "pursuant to section 69 of the County Courts Act 1984"

i) in respect of the period after the notice terminating the tenancy has come to an end, mesne profits should be sought. This is because during that time, the landlord is claiming there is no longer a tenancy and that rent payments would no longer be appropriate

j) a statement of truth at the end of the form

There is no need to dress this information up in legalese. A laymen's attempt to make documents read as if they were drafted by lawyers almost always result in an embarrassingly ungrammatical and pompous mess. Ordinary language, the simpler the better, is the best course to take. Indeed the Civil Procedure Rules now mean plain, simple and ordinary language is to be preferred

Adding some hypothetical facts to the tenancy of 41a Wilson Road and assuming it had been let to John Skinner, Jack Heffer and James Rooker:

At the end of the yearly term these tenants continued occupation of the property. They hold a succession of late night parties and neighbours complain to Mrs Healey. She serves the appropriate notice and commences possession proceedings. These are the Particulars of Claim she might use to commence an action at the end of May 2000.

IN THE BOW COUNTY COURT   CASE NO.

B E T W E E N

ANGELA H HEALEY   <u>Claimant</u>

and

(1) JOHN SKINNER
(2) JACK HEFFER
(3) JAMES ROOKER   <u>Defendants</u>

PARTICULARS OF CLAIM

---

1. The Claimant is the owner of the freehold of the property known as 41a Wilson Road, Stratford, London E15 ("the property").

2. By a tenancy agreement dated 31 January 1999 the Claimant granted to the Defendants a tenancy of the property for a term of one year from 1 February 1999 ("the tenancy").

3. Under the tenancy the Defendants pay a rent to the Claimant of £320 per week.

4. The tenancy was subject to the provisions of the Housing Act 1988.

5. The tenants have remained in possession of the property as statutory tenants under the provisions of the said Housing Act 1988.

6. On 1 May 1999 the Claimant served on the Defendants a notice pursuant to section 8 of the said Housing Act 1988 stating that possession would be sought pursuant to Grounds 12 and 13 of Schedule 2 to the said Housing Act 1988 not earlier than 17 May 1999.

7. The Claimant is entitled to possession on the basis of the said Grounds.

PARTICULARS

On 14 March 1999, 28 March 1999, 11 April 1999 and 25 April 1999 the Defendants have held noisy parties at the property which have lasted until at least 3 a.m. As a result of each of those parties occupants of adjoining properties have complained to the Claimant.

By covenant (x) of the said tenancy agreement, the Defendants covenanted not to permit or allow anything to be done on the premises which may be or become a nuisance or annoyance to the occupiers of any adjoining premises.

AND The Claimant claims:

(i) Possession of the property;
(ii) Mesne profits at the rate of £320 per week until possession of the property be given to the Claimant.

STATEMENT OF TRUTH
  * (I believe) (The Claimant believes) that the facts stated in this Claim Form are true.

  * I am duly authorised by the Claimant to sign this statement

Signed:...
  (Position (if not the Claimant)   ....)

* (Claimant) (Litigation friend) (Claimant's solicitor)

These particulars, of course, are the sort that are likely to be drafted by lawyers acting on Mrs Healey's behalf. There is no need for landlords doing their own to aspire to this particular style, but it may nonetheless be useful to have a professional model as a starting point.

The hearing
Where proceedings are commenced using the general procedure or the

"rent arrears" forms, the matter will be listed for a hearing. This will sometimes be before a circuit judge and sometimes a district judge. Circuit judges are one step higher up the judicial hierarchy than district judges. It makes little difference to the parties before which judge their case is listed except that district judge's lists are meant to be better managed resulting in less time spent waiting around at court.

If the tenant fails to put in any defence disputing the claim and does not attend the hearing, the landlord is unlikely to have any difficulty obtaining a possession order. But he will still have to turn up at court with all the relevant documents and any witnesses who can explain matters of which the landlord does not have first hand knowledge.

In many county courts the first hearing will be listed at the same time as a number of other cases. The expectation is that none of these cases will take longer than a few minutes. Beware, though, the court usher controls the order of the list in which it is called before the judge. If you irritate the court usher you can find yourself waiting a great deal longer!

If the tenant comes to court and raises matters that the judge feels could give him a defence, the hearing will be adjourned for a trial on a date when the court can set aside more time for it. Sometimes the court will not set such a date there and then. It may direct that the Defendant first serve a formal defence setting out his case.

After that the parties will have to send each other lists and copies of any relevant documents (known as disclosure and inspection) followed by written statements of their evidence. These statements should be more detailed than the particulars of claim and defence. These procedures can take weeks, even months. It is particularly frustrating for a landlord to have his possession claim delayed while this is done. Some judges will go out of their way to speed matters up.

It may be worthwhile asking the judge to make an order that the Defendant pay the rent until the hearing. The judge will normally only agree to such an order if he thinks it realistic to expect the Defendant to pay the money. If the tenant has persuaded the judge that he does have an arguable defence to the claim, it would be advisable for the landlord to consult a solicitor. There may well be a technical defence, such as a defect in a notice, to which there is no answer. If the landlord pursues a fatally flawed case through all the procedural steps to a trial he may end paying a substantial amount towards the tenant's legal costs. It is much better to have a professional appraisal of the case at an early stage.

At the trial the landlord bringing the claim will have to start his case by explaining to the judge what it is about and referring him to all the relevant documents. The landlord will then give evidence himself and have the opportunity to call any witnesses he wants. The tenant then has an opportunity to cross-examine the landlord and any of his witnesses. After that the tenant will give evidence. The landlord will have the opportunity to ask him questions - cross-examine him. After that the parties, starting (somewhat illogically) with the tenant, can each make a further speech to the judge saying why the judge should support his claim.

If a party is represented by a lawyer, that lawyer will do all the speech making and questioning for him. It should be remembered that when questions are asked either in examination-in-chief, or under cross-examination, the questioner (be it a lawyer or layman) should not follow the practice of American lawyers whereby one walks around the courtroom, gesticulating (and perhaps, accusing) wildly. There should always be respectful decorum, thus questions are asked from a stationary position, usually behind the desk or lectern, and without shouting.

The judge will then make a decision and he has a duty to give reasons for that decision. He may decide to make a possession order but suspend it on conditions, most commonly that the tenant pay off the arrears of rent and future rent. Either party can appeal against the judge's decision. However the rights of appeal are largely restricted to points of law and such a course should never be taken without legal advice.

Costs

When a person wins the case the court will normally make a costs order in that person's favour. This is directed primarily towards the costs of employing lawyers to fight the case. Where someone has won a case without a lawyer they can claim around £10 per hour for their time in preparing the case.

Whether or not a lawyer has been used, the landlord can claim out of pocket expenses for himself and witnesses and of course the court fee. If the costs are relatively small, as they should be if the order is made at the first hearing, the judge will usually assess a figure when making the possession order. If they are substantial the judge will order them to be subject to more detailed assessment, a process known as taxing. This is likely to result in the other side being ordered to pay considerably less than the litigant has to pay his own solicitor.

The solicitor is entitled to his agreed fee regardless of the amount assessed. If no fee was agreed with the solicitor, the litigant is entitled to insist on solicitor's bill being assessed. The solicitor should provide details of how this can be done when he submits his bill. Assessment in this situation is done on a different basis to one that decides how much the other party has to pay, and the landlord is still likely to be out of pocket.

To give an example, suppose a landlord has obtained a possession order on the basis of the tenants having committed various acts of nuisance at the property. They contested the case and it went to a full trial which lasted a whole day. The solicitors' bill for that and all the preliminary work might well be £2,000. The court might make an order that the tenants pay those costs.

However the tenants would have the right to have those costs assessed or taxed. Such an assessment might result in them only being required to pay £1,500, towards the £2,000 the landlord would have to pay his own solicitors. If the landlord thought his solicitors' bill was too much he could apply to have it assessed. It is unlikely that it would be reduced to anything like as low a figure as the tenants would have to pay. It might well be assessed on this basis as £1,800.

In practice the chances are that a tenant against whom a costs order is made is unlikely to pay them, just as he is unlikely to pay any arrears of rent or damages. If there is a surety, it should be possible to recover the costs against that person although ultimately it may be necessary to bring a separate court action to do so. If the other party is granted legal aid the court will usually make a costs order, but prohibit the winner from attempting to enforce it unless he obtains the court's permission to do so. This permission will only be granted where the other person's financial position has improved considerably since he was granted legal aid.

It might be worthwhile applying for permission a few years later if the tenant had been a student at the time of the court order, subsequently gets his qualification and obtains a good job. Alternatively, the tenant may have inherited a large amount of money from a relative, or even won the lottery!

The landlord can make the application in the six years following the making of the order. In practice this is rarely done if only because after litigation the parties do not usually keep in touch with other and the landlord will not know what has happened to the tenant.

Legal Aid (or Public Funding)
First, the term "legal aid" is technically obsolete, having been replaced by "public funding" under the Access to Justice Act 1999. The Legal Aid Board has also been renamed the Legal Services Commission. Second, whilst "public funding" should be the new nomenclature, the author, other lawyers, the media and general public and, even judges, continue to use the old terms.

There are two criteria for being eligible for legal aid (that is to satisfy the Legal Services Commission): the merits of the case and one's financial position. Most solicitors will provide an initial consultation without charging, during which they will advise whether it is worth making a legal aid application. The solicitor will be able to give a preliminary view on whether the case is meritorious enough for legal aid to be appropriate.

Financial eligibility is related to income and savings. An income and savings above certain limits mean the person will not be eligible at all. A lower income or savings will mean a contribution will have to be paid towards the legal aid. The relevant levels are frequently altered. From the income figure expenditure which relate to matters such as housing and travel to work can be disregarded.

In some circumstances where legal aid is granted and property is recovered, the Legal Services Commission will have a right to so much of that property as is needed to repay the fees the Commission has paid to the solicitor. The solicitor will explain this in detail when the legal aid application is made.

If a person has legal aid and loses the case, the normal rule that the loser pays the winner's costs will not usually not apply. In some circumstances this of itself can prove an even better reason for being legally aided than the advantages of having representation by a solicitor.

Recovering costs against an opponent who has been granted legal aid
If an assisted person loses the case then the court will only make an order for any costs to be recovered against him if, having had regard to all the circumstances, it is appropriate to do so. The circumstances under

which the court will pay most attention are the means of the assisted person. An inquiry may be made at Court where the party can be asked whether he can pay a certain sum per month (e.g.£10 per month for x months), in addition the court is likely to examine the conduct of the assisted person (e.g. did he behave unreasonably, etc).

In most scenarios, the court will make an order for the sum of money against the assisted person, however the sum is not to be enforced without the leave of the court. If, during the six years since the costs order was made an assisted person's financial resources significantly improve, an application can be made to the court to enforce the costs order. This is commonly referred to as a "football pools order"; because it was usually only if a person won the football pools that he would have the funds to pay. Perhaps by the next edition of this book the order will be known as the "Lottery order".

Obviously, in practice, a landlord will often be unable to determine the means of a tenant after he has moved out of the landlord's property. Landlords and tenants should be aware, however, that an assisted person will not be protected against all of a costs order if he takes steps and acts beyond the scope of the legal aid certificate he was granted. Thus, if a tenant makes a counterclaim against a landlord where, in fact, he has only been given the scope to defend the landlord's action; he is not protected from paying the landlord's costs in defending a counterclaim.

Legal Aid and Landlords
A landlord is entitled to apply for legal aid. However, in reality, the possibility of attaining help is reduced as a landlord's financial resources (disposable income and capital) will usually place him above the legal aid threshold for assistance. It should be remembered, however, that the property which is the subject matter of the (legal) dispute should be disregarded in calculating the landlord's capital, and the value of the landlord's only or principal dwelling should also be disregarded

Whilst these factors are still likely to place the landlord beyond the criteria to make him eligible for legal aid, a resident landlord may be in a different position.

Enforcement
Once a court has made an order for possession there is no guarantee that the tenant will leave immediately or even by the latest date the judge

had allowed him to remain. Once that last date has expired if the tenant remains in possession, the landlord has to obtain a warrant of possession from the court office. (It is not possible to obtain this in advance of that date in anticipation of the tenants not leaving when they ought to.) To obtain this warrant it is necessary to fill in another form (N325) and pay a further fee of £80. The bailiff will normally then set a date a few weeks' hence when the tenant will be evicted. He will visit the tenant first to give him warning of the application.

Once the tenant has been evicted the landlord would be well advised to immediately change the locks on the property and if necessary board it up. There is, surprisingly, little sanction against a tenant who breaks back in after being evicted.

Applications by tenants who have hitherto completely ignored the proceedings are sometimes made a day or two before a warrant is due to be enforced. Such an application can in certain circumstances even be made without the landlord having any opportunity to present his case. These applications often succeed largely because of the desire of the courts to avoid the social problems caused by making people homeless if at all possible. The result will be a wait of several further weeks before the landlord can actually get possession, however feeble the tenant's case. To say such delays are immensely frustrating for the landlord is an understatement.

Where there is a monetary judgement there are a number of ways in which a landlord can attempt to enforce this. The most effective is often an attachment of earnings order. (The procedure in respect of such enforcement is outside the scope of this book.)

From the tenant's perspective

Claims by tenants

Disrepair and harassment are the two main basis for tenants making claims against their landlords. If a landlord has physically evicted a tenant from a property, then it is likely that tenant will be able to obtain an order for very substantial damages. The tenant may be able to obtain an order known as an injunction requiring the landlord to let him back into the premises. Similarly in disrepair cases it may be possible to obtain an injunction requiring the landlord to carry out repairs. Obtaining these remedies is extremely complex and is not practical without the help of a solicitor.

Claiming damages is considerably more intricate than claiming rent arrears. It is often difficult to establish whether the tenant is entitled to anything at all. If he is entitled, assessing damages is much more difficult than merely stating that rent arrears at say £50 per week over ten weeks have built up. For this reason it is probably a good idea for tenants who bring such claims to seek the advice of a solicitor, or at the very least an advice bureau, before doing so.

However where the claim is only for a small amount, perhaps the landlord's initial failure to repair the roof has resulted in water leaking onto and spoiling a rug owned by the tenant, it might be worth bringing a claim without incurring the expense of a solicitor. Legal aid is unlikely to be available if the value of the claim is less than around £1,500. If the amount claimed is less than £3,000, the case is likely to be referred to the Small Claims Track which is a relatively informal hearing. Such claims can be commenced using form N1 if the tenant can give the precise amount claimed. An order for costs, other than the court fee, will not be made when a claim has been referred to arbitration because of the small amount of money involved.

When a landlord makes a possession claim, the tenant may be entitled to make a claim of his own against the landlord, a counterclaim. The forms the court will send him notifying him of the landlords claim will, unless the landlord uses the special procedure, ask if he wishes to make a counterclaim. If the tenant decides to deal with this without instructing a solicitor, he should set out in straight-forward language the basis for this. He will then eventually get the same opportunity to present his claim as the landlord.

Claims by landlords

A tenant faced with a possession claim made by a landlord but who wants to stay in position should seek the advice of a solicitor, or at the very least an advice bureau, about whether or not there is any potential defence. Often an experienced eye will pick up technicalities that can defeat or at least substantially delay the landlord's claim. Many solicitors make no charge for an initial interview. In practice tenants, generally being poorer than landlords, are far more likely to be eligible for legal aid.

If the claim is based upon rent arrears it is important for the tenant to attend court. There may not be any real defence to the claim but, particularly if there are less than three months' arrears, the court may be persuaded not to make a possession order if the rent and something towards the arrears is paid regularly in future. Last minute applications by tenants to stave off the enforcement of possession are discussed earlier. Whilst such applications can succeed, to rely on one doing so is most unwise. Many judges will be most unsympathetic to anyone who has been unnecessarily slow in responding to the proceedings.

Tenants, like anyone else faced with a legal claim, should do all they can to protect their position at the earliest possible moment. Likewise once an order for possession has been made, it is advisable to start looking for somewhere else to live. Leaving it to the last possible moment is virtually asking to be made homeless. Sometimes the local authority will be obliged to rehouse a person who has been the subject of a possession order. A tenant who feels this might be a possibility in his case should consult the housing department of the relevant authority as soon as is possible.

Most authorities will not rehouse a person if that person has become "intentionally homeless" (this includes leaving, even after a court order). Often then, and unfortunately, it means the only way in which one can be rehoused is to remain in the property, even after a possession order is made, and wait to be removed.

Legal Aid and Tenants

Whereas for a landlord, it is usually his financial position that will make him ineligible for legal aid. For a tenant, the difficult hurdle is the "merits of the case". A tenant, when applying for legal aid will need to show that he has a reasonable prospect of success in defending the landlord's action.

Once again, a solicitor should be consulted as soon as is possible. This is for two reasons. First, the solicitor will be able to assess the merits of the case. Secondly, the solicitor is in a better position to apply for emergency legal aid (if there is insufficient time for the application to be in writing). If a tenant has insufficient time to see a solicitor before the hearing or is still awaiting the decision of the Legal Services Commission, he should attend court and ask for an adjournment whilst the legal aid position is being considered.

To increase the chances of being granted an adjournment and, as a matter of courtesy, the tenant should inform the other side of his need for an adjournment and preferably, receive the other sides' consent to such a course. Obviously, it is always in the tenant's interests to gain an adjournment as this means he may remain in possession of the property until the final hearing. For this reason, Courts and Judges are often reticent to grant an adjournment. To have the best chance of success in gaining an adjournment, in these circumstances, the following should be shown:

> *a) the reason for the adjournment – so that legal aid may be considered*
>
> *b) a good reason why matters and/or applications have been unable to progress already – why the delay until the hearing*
>
> *c) that the other side had knowledge of the request for the adjournment*
>
> *d) that the tenant has a good prospect of defending the action*
>
> *e) that the tenant is willing to pay rent during the duration of the adjournment, and if there are any rent arrears, a willingness by the tenant to pay some of them*

Obviously, if the landlord has agreed the need for an adjournment, and the length of the adjournment, a judge will be far less likely to intervene in the parties' agreement.

As we have already noted, if a tenant has been granted legal aid but loses the case, an order will usually be made for the tenant to pay the costs that the landlord has incurred, except that the order cannot be enforced without leave of the court.

11

HUMAN RIGHTS - THE NEW LANDSCAPE

Unlike the rest of this book, this Chapter is not split into what should now be familiar - the distinct parts of "From the Landlord's" or "From the Tenant's" Perspective. The reason is threefold. Firstly, in this area, perhaps more than any other, it is necessary to appreciate both perspectives - the impact of the Convention rights is both a two-way and a balancing process. By splitting this up parties may fail to appreciate the proper outlook one should have. Secondly, it is only after litigation has begun that these rights are considered. Once litigation has started, parties should be encouraged to be as objective as possible - to "see the other sides' viewpoint". Thirdly, and the least compelling reason, is that as Human Rights provide a new landscape to be explored, there is nothing wrong in making this "new" chapter different.

On the 2nd October 2000, the Human Rights Act came into force. This now guarantees certain fundamental human rights. Some of these rights are inalienable (that is cannot be restricted in any way, for example the right to life). Others, though, are rights that can, in certain circumstance, be restricted or interfered with (for example, the right to associate can be restricted to prevent terrorist activities or public order offences). Some of the rights enshrined in the Act are applicable in the context of Landlord and Tenant. These are:

- · Article 8 - Everybody has the right to respect for private and family life, his home and his correspondence
- · Housing rights under Article 1 of Protocol 1 - every person is entitled to the peaceful enjoyment of his possessions
- · Article 6 - the right to a fair trial
- · Article 14 - freedom from discrimination
- · Article 3 - freedom from torture, inhuman or degrading treatment

It is important to remember that the application of human rights does not specifically apply as between individuals, but only in the relationship between individuals and the State. It is unlawful for any public authority to act in a manner that is incompatible with a convention right. A "public authority" is not defined in a positive manner in the Act except to say that the term includes a court or tribunal.

It is clear, though, that the concept of a public authority will include all bodies which are obviously public in nature, such as government departments, local government, local authorities, prisons, police officers, immigration officers, and courts and tribunals. All of these bodies will, save in very specific scenarios, act unlawfully if they act in a way which is inconsistent with the Convention.

Where both parties are private individuals (for example a landlord and tenant matter) human rights are applicable where a public authority becomes involved. Thus, if a dispute between a landlord and tenant goes to court, that court (as a public authority) cannot exclude or avoid the impact of a Convention right (such as the right to a fair trial).

Each of the Convention rights (applicable to landlord and tenant matters) will be discussed in turn.

Article 8

The essential objective of Article 8 is to protect an individual against arbitrary interference with their private and family life and their home. In March 2001, for example, a man who had been ordered to demolish a £750,000 house that he built without full planning permission was told by a planning inspector that he could keep the property as knocking it down would violate his human rights to his family life and his home. The protection against interference also has the effect of obliging the State to protect an individual's Article 8 rights even where the interference does not emanate from the State, but as from another private person.

Article 8 provides:

(1) Everyone has the right to respect for his private and family life, his home and his correspondence

(2) There shall be no interference by a public authority with the exercise of this right except such as is in accordance with the law and is necessary in a democratic society in the interests of national security, public safety or the economic

well-being of the country, for the prevention of disorder or crime, for the protection of health or morals, or for the protection of the rights and freedoms of others

Paragraph (1) provides the right, Paragraph (2) sets out the exceptions and limitations to the right.

Under Article 8(1) The word "home" includes any premises or shelter used by a person as his home in which he has a legal interest. The courts have also defined home in various ways. It has been defined as a continuous residence with no intention to establish home elsewhere and has even been extended to include the place where a person intends to live There remains, however, no general right to have a home or be provided with housing.

Under Article 8(2) the restrictions mean there is never an absolute right to respect a person's home or one's private and family life. Public authorities (defined above) have permission under paragraph (2) to restrict the provision of the right under paragraph (1) providing four requirements are met:

(1) the ground for interference is "in accordance with the law"
(2) the interference is to pursue a legitimate aim (national security, public safety, economic well-being of the UK, prevention of disorder or crime, protection of health or morals, protection of rights and freedoms of others)
(3) the interference is necessary
(4) the interference is proportionate to the legitimate aim

The requirement of proportionality is usually the most problematic to consider. In determining whether an interference is "proportionate" several assessments can be made. Namely, whether there are sufficient reasons for the action needed to be taken, whether there are safety measures in place that prevents, or limits, potential abuses; and whether the rights of the parties have been properly considered.

The State is not obligated, under Article 8, to give a landlord the right to recover on request a house that he has let. The tenant also has his rights. Consequently, all that can be done is to make an objective assessment of each parties' rights. As a result, in the area of landlord and tenant,frequently the notion of procedural fairness - for example whether statutes and procedures have been followed - is the only one likely to be considered. Since, if landlord and tenant statutes and procedures are followed (for example, relevant grounds and notice periods in an eviction) it will usually follow that the interference is "in accordance with the law"; "protects the rights and freedoms of [for example, the landlord]"; is "necessary" and is "proportionate" as the laws and procedures provide adequate safeguards.

It is perhaps for this reason that, in the main, an argument by a landlord or tenant solely under Article 8 is likely to fail if procedures and statutes have been followed. Furthermore, it follows, that where there does lie an argument under Article 8 there should be arguments under other aspects of English law - for example, relevant notice periods and grounds being abused.

As an example whilst it may be argued that a tenant's eviction will interfere with his right to occupy his home (Article 8), if the eviction has been performed by going through the appropriate procedures (notices and time-limits, etc) it is equally right to argue that as the tenancy has properly come to an end (by expiry of time or notice) the premises no longer qualify as a home and so Article 8 is inapplicable and of no relevance.

Alternatively it might be argued that eviction being properly followed complies with Article 8(2). All in all, therefore, Article 8 is unlikely to be of any further assistance to landlords in gaining possession of their property, and to tenants in preventing a landlord's interference.

Article 1 of Protocol 1

Article 1 of the First Protocol states:
Every natural or legal person is entitled to the peaceful enjoyment of his possessions. No one shall be deprived of his possessions except in the public interest and subject to the conditions provided for by law and by the general principles of international law.

The preceding provisions shall not, however, in any way impair the right of a State to enforce such laws as it deems necessary to control the use of property in accordance with the general interest or to secure the payment of taxes or other contributions or penalties.

The aim, here, is to protect a person's existing possessions. Although it is not explicitly stated, the term "possessions" guarantees, in substance, the right of property (it includes land, contractual rights and leases, shares, patents and debts). Thus, a landlords' interest in his property, and the interests of a tenant are covered.

What Article 1 of Protocol 1 does not do, however, is guarantee a right to acquire "possessions". Unfortunately, though, Article 1 of the First Protocol is primarily concerned with simply protecting individuals against the actions of public authorities. As a result (just like the application of other Convention rights) it will be of extremely limited use and application in the realms of private matters, such as in private landlord and tenant matters. Its application is likely to only be adopted where a public authority is involved - for example in court, or in council housing decisions (outside the scope of this book).

Any deprivation occurring to a person's property (the peaceful enjoyment of his possessions) must be "subject to the conditions provided for by law". In other words, there must subsist a proper basis for the deprivation in domestic law. In general, for there to be a proper basis, the law must be accessible and sufficiently certain, and which protects against arbitrariness. Thus, even if it is shown that Protocol 1, Article 1, has been violated, interference, deprivation or control will not be deemed to be violated it if it has been done "in the public interest" or "to enforce such laws [as the State] deems necessary to control the use of property in accordance with the general interest".

A court will, in determining the level of interference that it finds is permissible against the right of peaceful enjoyment of possessions, apply a balancing exercise similar to the one used in Article 8 scenarios. That is, the test of "proportionality" between the aim that is pursued and the means employed.

Thus, any interference or violation with the fundamental right of a person to the "peaceful enjoyment of his possessions" must achieve a fair balance between this right and the "general interest" of the community and state. Any court or tribunal, when deciding issues under Protocol 1, Article 1 is granted what is known as a "margin of appreciation" in deciding what the "general interest" demands.

A useful interpretation was given in the case of <u>Mellacher v Austria</u> ((1989) 12 EHRR 391), it was said that "the second paragraph [in Article

1 of Protocol 1] reserves to states the right to enact such laws as they deem necessary to control the use of property in accordance with the general interest. Such laws are especially common in the field of housing, which in our modern societies is a central concern of social and economic policies. In order to implement such policies, the legislature must have a wide margin of appreciation both with regard to the existence of a problem of public concern warranting measures of control and as to the choice of the detailed rules for the implementation of such measures".

Readers should not get confused between Article 8 and Article 1, Protocol 1. Article 8 protects the right to occupy the home peacefully and enjoy its comforts without arbitrary interference; Article 1, Protocol 1 protects the property right in a home.

Article 6

Article 6 concerns the right to a fair trial. It is divided into three sections. Only section 1 is of relevance here, sections 2 and 3 being exclusively relevant to criminal law.

Article 6 states:

(1) In the determination of his civil rights and obligations or of any criminal charge against him, everyone is entitled to a fair and public hearing within a reasonable time by an independent and impartial tribunal established by law. Judgment shall be pronounced publicly but the press and public may be excluded from all or part of the trial in the interests of morals, public order or national security in a democratic society, where the interests of juveniles or the protection of the private life of the parties so require, or to the extent strictly necessary in the opinion of the court in special circumstances where publicity would prejudice the interests of justice.

Article 6 will only be relevant to landlords and tenants if a matter goes to court. Article 6(1) should also be self-explanatory to most readers. The overriding obligation is to ensure that the court proceedings are fair and that justice is seen to be done. Generally speaking, matters that fall into this area include the right of each party to produce evidence, cross-examine the other party and make arguments and submissions to the judge.

The court is also under a duty to give reasons for any decision that it makes - so that a party is able to know and understand how the court came to its decision. In addition, for a fair-hearing to take place, the parties need to know the time and place of the court proceedings and have an opportunity to present their case. However, the mere fact that a party fails to attend the court will not necessarily mean that the hearing will not take place, otherwise justice could always be obstructed by an unwilling party.

The concept of "equality of arms" also falls within the ambit of Article 6. This requires that there be a fair balance between the opportunities afforded the parties involved in the dispute. Thus, for example, a defence witness should be allowed to be examined under the same conditions as a witness for the Claimant. In addition, each party should also have the right to be represented by a lawyer or if they choose not to be represented, to appear in person. They should also be permitted to cross-examine the other party's evidence and to present their arguments and submissions.

Article 6 provides for both landlords and tenants (and, indeed, any other citizen) the guarantees for a fair trial. Readers, though, should not forget the application of Article 8 as it too has an impact on procedural fairness. Article 8(2) provides the phrase "in accordance with the law". Accordingly, landlord and tenant disputes should be decided under English (and Welsh) law which prescribes the procedures to follow. Thus, as in many other areas, there is a significant overlap between Article 6 and Article 8.

Article 14

Article 14 provides a prohibition on discrimination. It provides:

> *The enjoyment of the rights and freedoms set forth in this Convention shall be secured without discrimination on any ground such as sex, race, colour, language, religion, political or other opinion, national or social origin, association with a national minority, property, birth or other status.*

Article 14 does not provide a general right to freedom from discrimination and so cannot be used on its own. It can only be utilised in conjunction with another right, where a party is arguing that another right has been violated (curiously, though, it does not need to be established that another right has been breached only that a matter falls within the scope of a provision other than Article 14).

Whilst this provision may apply to housing matters (for example a local housing authority refusing to provide housing to a certain race, minority or sex), it is unlikely to apply to the private landlord and tenant relationship.

Article 3
Article 3 provides that:
"No one shall be subjected to torture or to inhuman or degrading treatment or punishment".

The only likely possible application of Article 3 in the landlord and tenant relationship will be by the tenant. The only time it is envisaged that this may ever occur is where a landlord illegally evicts a tenant and, probably, by application of force. Obviously when this scenario occurs the tenant will also have an argument under the Protection from Eviction Act 1977 and perhaps also, providing such treatment has occurred on more than one occasion, the Protection from Harassment Act 1997.

Sometimes, however, human rights will provide greater protection, thus in a case in 1997 the European Court decided that removal of a person who was suffering under an incurable and terminal illness would amount to a breach of both Article 3 and, indeed, Article 2 (the right to life).

Conclusion
The Human Rights Act 1998 has afforded further protection to both landlords and tenants. However, in general, it has not provided sufficiently greater protection since English (and Welsh) law has already in place a large number of legal authorities and statutes to prevent abuses in most areas.

Landlords and tenants should be extremely wary to invoke any argument on human rights by itself. Indeed, it is doubtful whether, in most straight-forward private landlord and tenant relationships, there can be any argument under Human Rights alone. Even using human rights in conjunction with "traditional" law should entail caution.

Further advice should be always be sought from lawyers.

12

FORMS

Both landlords and tenants should be aware that most claim forms and replies can now be downloaded from the internet. The best source is at www.courtservice.gov.uk Once on this website click on "forms and leaflets" and then click on "housing matters". There should then appear a list of different documents which can be downloaded.

In order to read them, most require a package called Acrobat Reader. If your PC does not have this, it too can be downloaded from various sites on the web.

Once the form appears on the screen all that needs to be done is for the relevant fields to be typed in. The form cannot, however, be saved in its completed form so anyone using the forms for legal purposes should remember to print out a sufficient number of copies and keep at least one for safe-keeping.

Hard blank copies of most of the forms relating to landlord and tenant matters can also be purchased from legal stationers.

Notice of an assured shorthold tenancy

This notice is no longer necessary to create an assured shorthold tenancy. Any agreement after the 28 February 1997 will automatically create one, unless there is an explicit notice or agreement to the contrary. The notice is included here, so that any tenancy granted before 28 February 1997 can be checked to see whether an assured shorthold tenancy was properly created.

Notice of an assured shorthold tenancy

Housing Act 1988 section 20

· Please write clearly in black ink
· If there is anything you do not understand you should get advice from a solicitor or a Citizen's Advice bureau, before you agree to the tenancy.

· This landlord must give this notice to the tenant before the tenancy is granted.

· This document is important, keep it in a safe place.

To   ....

[name of proposed tenant, if a joint tenancy is being offered enter the names of the joint tenants]

You are proposing to take a tenancy of the dwelling house known as:-

....

....

from   /   /19   to   /   /19   *The tenancy must be for a term certain of at least six months*

2. This notice is to tell you that your tenancy is to be an assured shorthold tenancy. Provided you keep to the terms of the tenancy, you are entitled to remain in the dwelling for at least the first six months of the fixed period agreed at the start of the tenancy. At the end of this period, depending on the terms of the tenancy, the landlord may have the right to repossession if he wants.

3. The rent for this tenancy is the rent we have agreed. However, you have the right to apply to a rent assessment committee for a determination of the rent which the committee considers might reasonably have been obtained under the tenancy. If the committee considers (i) that there is a sufficient number of similar properties in the locality let on assured tenancies and that (ii) the rent we have agreed is significantly higher than the rent which might reasonably be obtained having regard to the level of the rents for other assured tenancies in the locality, it will determine a rent for the tenancy. That rent will be the legal maximum you can be required to pay from the date the committee directs. If the rent includes council tax, the rent determined by the committee will be inclusive of council tax.

To be signed by the landlord or his agent (someone acting for him). If there are joint landlords each must sign, unless one signs on behalf of the rest with their agreement.

Signed ....…...   [Name of landlord(s)]

....   [address of landlord(s)]

Tel: ....

If signed by agent, name and address of agent

Name of agent ....

Address of agent ....

Tel: ....

Date   /   /19

Special note for existing tenants

· Generally if you have a protected or statutory tenancy and you give it up to take a new

111

tenance in the same or other accommodation owned by the same landlord, that tenancy cannot be an assured tenancy. It can still be a protected tenancy.

· But if you currently occupy a dwelling which was let to you as a protected shorthold tenant, special rules apply.

· If you have an assured tenancy which is not a shorthold under the Housing Act 1988, you cannot be offered an assured tenancy of the same or other accommodation by the same landlord.

Tenancy agreement

This agreement is made on [date] between [landlord's name] (hereinafter called "the landlord") and [tenant's name] (hereinafter called "the tenant").

IT IS AGREED AS FOLLOWS:

The landlord will let and the tenants take the premises known as [address of premises] together with the fixtures, fittings, furniture and effects therein, which are listed in the attached inventory for a term of [length] (hereinafter called "the term") commencing on [date] at a rent of [amount] per [week or month] to be paid in advance on [rent day or date].

The tenants agree to and will:

(i) Pay the rent on the days and in the manner aforesaid, making the first payment on [date]

(ii) Pay to the landlord a deposit of [amount] as security for any loss including legal costs, which may for this purpose be assessed on an indemnity basis, which the landlord may suffer by reason of the tenant's failure to pay rent and observe the other covenants herein

(iii) Pay for all gas and electricity consumed or supplied on or to the premises (including all fixed and standing charges) and all charges for maintenance and use of a telephone on the premises during the term

(iv) Keep the interior of the premises clean and tidy and in as good a state of repair and decorative condition as at the beginning of the term, reasonable wear and tear excepted

(v) Keep the contents clean

(vi) Not damage or injure the premises

(vii) Not remove any of the contents from the premises

(viii) Replace any of the contents which may be destroyed or damaged so as to be unusable other than through fair wear and tear with others of similar value and appearance

(ix)[If appropriate] Keep the garden clean and tidy and in a proper state of cultivation and prevent it from becoming overgrown

(x) Not exhibit any poster or notice so that it is visible from outside the premises

(xi) Not permit or allow anything to be done on the premises which may be or become a nuisance or annoyance to the landlord or the occupiers of any adjoining premises or which may render the landlord's insurance of the premises void or voidable or increase the rate of such premium

(xii) Not carry on any trade, business or profession on the premises nor receive paying guests, but use the premises only as a private residence

(xiii) Not use or allow the premises to be used for any illegal or immoral purpose

(xiv) Not make any noise or play any radio, television set, musical instrument, hi-fi system, record player, tape player, stereo or similar device at the premises between 11 p.m. and 8 a.m. so as to be audible outside the premises

(xv) Not allow more than [number appropriate to type of property] people to reside or stay overnight at the premises

(xvi) Not keep any animal at the premises

(xvii) Not block or cause any blockage to the drains and pipe gutters and channels in or about the premises

(xviii) Not assign, underlet or part with possession of the whole or any part of the premises

(xix) Permit the landlord and the landlord's agents at reasonable times in daylight by appointment to enter the premises during the last 28 days of the term with prospective tenants and during any part of the term with prospective purchasers of the landlord's interest in the premises

(xx) Notify the landlord forthwith in writing of any defects in the premises as soon as practicable after the tenant has become aware of such defects

(xxi) At the end of the term:

(a) Yield up the premises and the contents in such state of repair and condition as shall be in accordance with the tenant's obligations under this agreement

(b) Make good or pay for the repair or replacement of such of the contents as have been broken, lost or damaged during the term

(c) Pay for washing (including ironing and pressing) of all linen and for the washing and cleaning (including ironing and pressing) of all blankets, curtains and similar items which have been soiled during the tenancy

(d) Leave the contents in the rooms and places in which they were at the commencement of the term

[If there is more than one tenant] And each tenant shall be responsible for the breach of any obligation hereunder by any other tenant as if he had broken the same himself, and shall be liable for the full rent regardless of any failure to contribute to the same by the other tenants or the fact that he or she is no longer living at the premises

The landlord agrees to and will:

(i) Pay and indemnify the tenant against all council tax (or other rates) assessments and outgoings and all water and sewerage charges in respect of the premises

(ii) Keep the premises (though not the contents) insured against fire, flood, storm and similar risks

(iii) Permit the tenant, so long as he or she pays the rent and performs his or her obligations under this agreement, quietly to use and enjoy the premises during the term without any interruption from the landlord or any person rightfully claiming under or in trust for the landlord

(iv) Return to the tenant any rent payable for any period during which the premises may have been rendered uninhabitable by fire or any other risk against which the landlord may have insured

(v) Upon the yielding up of possession of the premises by the tenant at the end of the term return to the tenant the deposit (less any proper deductions which may then be due from the tenant to the landlord as a result of any breach by the tenant of any of the tenant's obligations under this agreement) with simple interest calculated at the rate of 5% per annum

If:

(i) Any part of the rent is in arrears for more than 14 days whether formally demanded or not or

(ii) If there is any breach of any of the tenant's obligations under this agreement or

(iii) If the premises are, without the agreement of the landlord, left unoccupied for a continuous period in excess of four weeks, the landlord may re-enter the premises and thereupon the tenancy created by this agreement will determine, but without prejudice to any other rights and remedies of the landlord

Signed by the landlord ....

Landlord's signature witnessed by [name and address]

Signed by witness..............

Signed by the tenant...........

Tenant's signature witnessed by [name and address]

Signed by witness..............

[NB: This is for use where the tenancy is for a fixed term and is furnished. It can be adapted fairly quickly and easily where the terms are to be different. It should have the effect of creating an assured shorthold tenancy (providing it relates to an agreement after 28 February 1997)]

Notice to an assured shorthold tenant that the landlord requires possession

To [tenant's name] of [tenant's address]

I [or if notice is given by agent I [name of agent] giving notice on behalf of your land-lord(s)] [landlord's name] of [landlord's address] give you notice that I [or the landlord] require possession by virtue of section 21 of the Housing Act 1988 of the property at [property address] on or before the day on which a complete period of your tenancy expires after [date at least two months after service of this notice] and that if you do not give up possession of the said dwelling-house to me [or the landlord] on or before that date, I [or the landlord] will commence court proceedings for possession.

Date ....

Signed ....

[If appropriate The name and address of the agent who served this notice is.........]

Notice to quit addressed to tenant

To [tenant's name] of [tenant's address]

I/We [or if notice is given by agent I/we [name of agent] giving notice on behalf of your landlord(s)] [landlord's name] of [landlord's address] give you notice to quit and deliver up possession to him of [address of let premises] on [date] or the day on which a complete period of your tenancy expires next after the end of four weeks from the service of this notice

Date ....

Signed ....

[if appropriate The name and address of the agent who served this notice is.............]

Information for tenant
1. If the tenant of licensee does not leave the dwelling, the landlord or licensor must get an order for possession from the court before the tenant or licensee can lawfully be evict-ed. The landlord or licensor cannot apply for such an order before the notice to quit or notice to determine has run out.
2. A tenant or licensee who does not know if he has any right to remain in possession after a notice to determine runs out can obtain advice from a solicitor. Help with all or part of the cost of legal advice and assistance may be available under the Legal Aid Scheme. He should also be able to obtain information from a Citizens' Advice Bureau, a Housing Aid Centre or a rent officer.

Notes

1. Notice to quit any premises let as a dwelling must be given at least four weeks before it is to take effect and it must be in writing (Protection from Eviction Act 1977, s5).

2. Where a notice to quit is given by a landlord to determine a tenancy of any premises let as a dwelling, the notice must contain this information (The Notices to Quit etc (Prescribed Information) Regulations 1988 (SI No 2201).

GLOSSARY

assignment: the transfer of a tenancy from one person to another

assured tenancy: a residential tenancy granted after 14 January 1989

bailiff: a court official whose task it is to enforce court orders including those for eviction (q.v.)

break clause: a provision in a tenancy that enables either the landlord or the tenant to terminate it before the term (q.v.) expires

Case 11 tenancy: a tenancy granted before 15 January 1989 where the landlord served a notice saying the property had previously been his home and that he intended living there again in the future

counterclaim: a claim made by the defendant (q.v.) in court proceedings

covenant: a term often used to describe the promises given in the lease by the landlord and the tenant

defence: the formal document filed by the defendant (q.v.) in court proceedings, may also contain a counterclaim (q.v.)

defendant: the person against whom court proceedings are brought, occasionally the term respondent is used instead

demised premises: the property that is the subject matter of a tenancy

deposit: a payment by a tenant to a landlord to secure the tenant's performance of his obligations including paying rent and not causing any damage

eviction: the act of removing a person from a property. If it is done without a court order it is almost certainly a wrongful eviction (q.v.)

exclusive possession: the right to occupy property to the exclusion of everyone else; this is the defining feature of a tenancy

fair rent: a rent assessed by a rent officer (q.v.) in respect of a tenancy subject to the Rent Act 1977

fixtures and fittings: things that although not an integral part of a property that are attached to it, unlike furniture which is removable, e.g fitted carpets, wallpaper. (Not rugs or unfitted wardrobes however heavy and difficult to move)

forfeiture: when a landlord decrees a tenancy has ended because the tenant has broken the terms of it or not paid the rent, and a forfeiture clause (q.v.) permits him to do so

forfeiture clause: a clause in a tenancy agreement saying the landlord is entitled to treat the tenant as having forfeited the lease if he breaks its terms or does not pay the rent.

freehold: absolute ownership of property. Most house owners are freeholders, but most flats are let on long leases (q.v.)

Ground 1 tenancy: tenancy granted after 14 January 1989, where the landlord served a notice saying the property had previously been his home or that he intended living there again in the future

ground rent: rent paid by a lessee under a long lease, usually of a nominal annual amount to the freeholder

Housing Act 1988: Act of Parliament under which Rent Acts (q.v.) were repealed in respect of tenancies subsequent to 14 January 1989 and by which another regime, generally less favourable to tenants, was substituted

Housing benefit: a form of social security administered by local authorities to help relatively poor people pay their rent

injunction: an order made by a court compelling someone to do something e.g. carry out repairs, or refrain from doing something e.g. harassing a tenant

joint and several liability: form of agreement under which two or more tenants are each liable in respect of the breaches of other tenants' as well as their own

"key money": alternative word for premium (q.v.) for a short term tenancy

lease: an agreement under which someone agrees to let another have exclusive possession (q.v.) of a property

Legal aid: government funding for lawyers to represent poorer people in legal proceedings

licence: agreement under which one person allows another to occupy property, but which does not amount to a tenancy (q.v.), usually because exclusive possession (q.v.) is not given

licensee: someone who is given a licence (q.v.) to occupy propert.

licensor: someone who licenses another person to occupy property

licence fee: the correct term for "rent" (q.v.) paid under a licence (q.v.)

*lodger:*person paying to live in another's home, almost always a licensee (q.v.)

long lease: usually refers to a lease of longer than 21 years. Usually rent under such a lease will be a nominal ground rent (q.v.) but a substantial premium will be required for the grant or assignment of such a lease

mesne profits: sum payable by a tenant who has continued living at a property after his tenancy has ended, usually equivalent to the rent he was paying before the tenancy ended

monthly tenancy: a periodic tenancy (q.v.) where rent is payable monthly

mortgage: the right over property given by an owner who is leant money, usually by a building society or a bank, on the security of that property

mortgagee: person granting the mortgage (q.v.) in exchange for being lent money, i.e. the property owner

mortgagor: person or institution) lending money secured on property

notice to quit: a notice served by a landlord or a tenant on the other party announcing their intention of ending a tenancy

particulars of claim: a plaintiff's (q.v.) written statement of what he is alleging and claiming set out when he commences court proceedings

"paying guest": another term for lodger (q.v.)

periodic tenancy: tenancy which is not for a fixed term, but which is automatically renewed each time the tenant pays his rent for the period that rent covers, e.g. a week, month or quarter

plaintiff: person who commences court proceedings by making a claim, in some circumstances referred to as the applicant

possession order: order made by the court requiring a person to leave property

premium: payment made by a tenant in consideration of the grant or assignment of a tenancy. (Normally not required for residential tenancies where a market rent is paid) The substantial payment made when buying a long lease on a flat is a premium

protected shorthold tenancy: a tenancy granted after 14 January 1989 for a term in excess of six months, during which time the landlord cannot terminate the tenancy, and in respect of which the landlord has served the appropriate notice

protected tenancy: residential tenancy granted before 15 January 1989. Once the tenancy has expired or the landlord has served notice to quit (q.v.) it becomes a statutory tenancy (q.v.)

Protection from Eviction Act 1977: Act of Parliament which provides serious civil and criminal sanctions against a landlord who harasses or wrongfully evicts a tenant

rent: payment by a tenant in consideration for being able to occupy property for a certain period under a tenancy.

Rent Acts: series of Acts of Parliament culminating in the Rent Act 1977 under which tenants were given extensive security of tenure and rent control. Repealed in respect of most subsequent tenancies by Housing Act 1988 (q.v.)

Rent Assessment Committee: committee, usually chaired by a lawyer, which conducts most official rent assessment other than that which is the rent officer's (q.v.) responsibility

rent book: a book provided by the landlord but kept by the tenant which the landlord signs as a receipt for each payment of rent made by the tenant

rent officer: an official whose primary job is the setting of fair rents (q.v.) in respect of tenancies granted before 15 January 1989

restricted contract: a tenancy granted before 15 January 1989 under which the landlord and the tenant live in the same building

Section 20 notice: a notice that, before 28th February 1997, was compulsory in order to grant an assured shorthold tenancy. It was essential for the form to be completed correctly in order for it to be valid. Any tenancy granted after the 28th February 1997 is automatically an assured shorthold.

secure tenancy: a residential tenancy granted by a local authority

service licence: a licence (q.v.) granted to somebody to live in property, which is essential to enable that person to perform his employment duties

service occupancy: another term for a service licence (q.v.)

"sitting tenant": person who has acquired statutory protection particulary under the Rent Acts (q.v.) and cannot be removed by his landlord.

"squatter": a person who has moved into property without ever having the permission of anyone entitled to give him such permission

statutory assured tenancy: tenancy arising after an assured tenancy has ended

statutory tenancy: tenancy that arises after a protected tenancy (q.v.) has ended

subletting: the letting by a tenant of some or all of the demised premises (q.v.) to another tenant

surety: a person who agrees to pay a debt if the person, such as the tenant, principally liable should default on it

tenancy: an agreement under which one person, a landlord, grants to another, a tenant, the right to exclusive possession (q.v.) of property for a specified term or renewable period

term: the length of time for which a tenancy is granted

warrant of possession: the order given by the court to the bailiffs instructing them to evict, physically if necessary, people from property after a possession order (q.v.) has been made

weekly tenancy: a periodic tenancy (q.v.) where rent is payable weekly

wrongful eviction: the act of unlawfully evicting a person from a property. Evictions (q.v.) are normally only lawful if carried out by a bailiff pursuant to a court order

NOTES

If you have found this book useful you may also find other books by Fitzwarren Handbooks of interest.

The E-Commerce Handbook
Andrew Sparrow
A practical legal guide to doing business over the internet, including suggested terms and conditions, use of domain names and trademarks, advertising agreements, website development contracts, etc.

The Litigation Handbook
Anthony Reeves and Alan Matthews
A concise account of how the English civil courts operate. Contains valuable information to enable the reader to pursue - or defend - a simple claim in the county court.

The Elections Handbook
Ron Kendall
An in-depth account of UK election procedures. An invaluable guide for electoral staff or for anyone running for public office.

Fitzwarren Handbooks provide helpful jargon-free guidance on a number of legal subjects. Written by professionals but with the layman in mind, the books are presented in a clear, easy-to-read style invaluable to lay persons and yet with sufficient depth to be of assistance to lawyers and other professionals working in relevant areas.